A PHOTOG

MINERALS, ROCKS AND FOSSILS

JOHN L. ROBERTS

NEW HOLLAND

This edition published in 2001 by
New Holland Publishers (UK) Ltd
London • Cape Town • Sydney • Auckland

Garfield House	80 McKenzie Street	14 Aquatic Drive
86 Edgware Road	Cape Town 8001	Frenchs Forest, NSW 2086
London W2 2EA	South Africa	Australia

First published in 1998

ISBN 1 85974 939 9

Commissioning editor: Jo Hemmings

Edited and designed by D & N Publishing, Membury Business Park
Lambourn Woodlands, Hungerford, Berkshire

Reproduction by Modern Age Repro House Limited, Hong Kong
Printed and bound in Malaysia by Times Offset (M) Sdn Bhd

10 9 8 7 6 5 4 3

Front cover photograph: Agate
Back cover photograph: Malachite and Azurite
Title page photograph: Nail-head Spar

Acknowledgements
Nearly all the photographs illustrating this book were taken by the author,
who would like to thank the following people and institutions for allowing
him access to their collections of mineral, rock and fossil specimens: Don
Shelley of the Orcadian Stone Company, Main Street, Golspie, Sutherland,
whose museum and workshop is open to the public, and Anne Shelley for
her hospitality; Richard Widdowson, a supplier of mineral and fossil specimens by mail order (catalogue from R.G. Widdowson, 32 Oak Road, Scar-
borough, North Yorkshire YO12 4AR); Richard Tayler Minerals, Byways,
20 Burstead Close, Cobham, Surrey KT11 2NL (catalogue available by
post); Giles Droop and his colleagues in the Department of Geology of the
University of Manchester; and Stuart Allison of the University of St Andrews
in Scotland. Duplicate 35mm transparencies of the photographs illustrating
this book are available from Landform Slides, 38 Borrow Road, Lowestoft,
Suffolk NR32 3PN, who supplied the following photographs: dune bedding
(page 46), desert sand (page 46), and pseudotachylyte breccia (page 124).

Contents

CONTINENTAL CRUST

HORNBLEND

QUARTZ

FELDSPAR

Preface

This introduction to minerals, rocks and fossils is intended for amateur naturalists who want a straightforward guide to their identification in the field. More than two thousand minerals are known to science, but many are extremely rare. This guide concentrates upon the minerals most likely to be encountered in the field by the amateur naturalist. Equally, while the fossil record is very incomplete, it now includes well over 150,000 different species. Only the major groups of fossils are described in this guide as they are an important feature of sedimentary rocks. The order in which the minerals, rocks and fossils are presented in this book follows conventionally adopted sequences.

Most rocks making up the solid fabric of the Earth are mere aggregates of mineral grains, but they reveal a history of past changes in the Earth's geography and climate. Indeed geology, of all the branches of natural history, perhaps leaves most to the imagination, even though it seems rooted in the most solid of evidence. Rocks are best examined in the field, where exposures often display the rocks' structural features on a large scale, revealing much about their nature and origin. Their texture and mineral composition can then be studied, preferably on a weathered surface, using a hand lens of good quality with a magnification of ×8 or ×10.

While exact names can often be given to mineral and fossil specimens of good enough quality, identifying rocks by name in the field is much less precise, especially when dealing with igneous rocks. But there is much more to geology as a branch of natural history than the mere collection and naming of specimens, whether they be minerals, rocks or fossils. The words of Charles Lyell, writing in 1838, cannot be bettered. He asked:

Of what materials is the earth composed, and in what manner are these materials arranged? These are the inquiries with which geology is occupied ... Such investigations appear at first sight to relate exclusively to the mineral kingdom ... But, in pursuing these researches, we soon find ourselves led on to consider the successive changes which have taken place in the former state of the earth's surface ... and the causes which have given rise to these changes ... What is still more singular and unexpected, we soon become engaged in researches into the history of the animal creation, and of the various tribes of animals and plants which have, at different periods of the past, inhabited the globe.

Identifying a rock can therefore be just the first step on a wider journey of discovery, which leads the amateur naturalist into the byways of geological history. Its study tells us not only how the land was constructed over vast eons of geological time, giving rise to the wide variety of different rocks we now see exposed at its surface, but how the physical landscape was sculpted from the underlying rocks by the weather. By looking at rocks in the field, and determining their nature and origin, the amateur naturalist will gain a greater appreciation of the natural environment, and come to understand how the landscape reveals the nature of the underlying geology.

4

Geological time-scale

Era	Period	Age
CENOZOIC ERA	QUATERNARY	**1.65 million years**
	TERTIARY	**65 MY**
MESOZOIC ERA	CRETACEOUS	**146 MY**
	JURASSIC	**208 MY**
	TRIASSIC	**245 MY**
UPPER PALAEOZOIC ERA	PERMIAN	**290 MY**
	(Pennsylvanian) CARBONIFEROUS (Mississippian)	**363 MY**
	DEVONIAN	**409 MY**
LOWER PALAEOZOIC ERA	SILURIAN	**439 MY**
	ORDOVICIAN	**510 MY**
	CAMBRIAN	**570 MY**
PRECAMBRIAN ERA	PROTEROZOIC	**2500 MY**
	ARCHEAN	**4600 MY**
ORIGIN OF THE EARTH		

MINERALS

Minerals are chemical elements or compounds, occurring naturally as inorganic substances in a crystalline state. Their atoms are always arranged in a very regular manner, characteristic of each mineral species, so forming a **crystal lattice**. This gives them a definite chemical composition, which only varies within certain limits as different elements substitute for one another as the result of **solid solution**. Minerals with the same chemical composition, but differing in internal structure and therefore crystal form, are known as **polymorphs**.

Rock-forming minerals Apart from limestone, dolomite and salt deposits, nearly all rocks are composed of silicate minerals, since silicon (Si) and oxygen (O) are the two most common elements in the Earth's crust. They combine in various ways with aluminium (Al), sodium (Na), potassium (K), calcium (Ca), iron (Fe) and magnesium (Mg), along with less common elements like beryllium (Be), boron (B), chlorine (Cl), fluorine (F), lithium (Li), chromium (Cr), manganese (Mn), strontium (Sr), titanium (Ti) and zirconium (Zr). Hydroxyl ions (OH) and water of crystallization (H_2O) may also be present. Solid solution is a common feature in nearly all silicate minerals, which often vary in composition between two or more end-members, while still displaying much the same crystal form as they change in chemical composition.

Vein and ore minerals Quite apart from the rock-forming minerals, other minerals are formed by the opening of fractures or fissures in the Earth's crust, allowing hot but watery solutions to flow upwards from the depths. Such **hydrothermal solutions** are often chemically active, carrying material in solution, which crystallizes out as the temperature and pressure fall closer to the Earth's surface. The deposits formed in this way typically occur as sheet-like veins with parallel sides, cutting across their **country-rocks**.

Hydrothermal solutions may also impregnate the surrounding rocks with mineral matter or even replace these rocks by reacting with their constituent minerals, often in a very irregular manner.

Crystals Minerals sometimes occur as well-developed crystals bounded by **crystal faces**. The faces always lie at an exact angle to one another, changing only slightly as solid solution alters the chemical composition of the mineral itself. Such external regularity merely reflects how the constituent atoms make up the crystal lattice of the mineral.

Cubic minerals These have highly symmetrical lattices and occur as six-sided **cubes** with square faces, eight-sided **octahedra** with triangular faces, twelve-sided **dodecahedra**, often with rhombic faces, and other forms with twenty-four or forty-eight faces.

Hexagonal and trigonal minerals These usually occur as parallel-sided **prisms** with six or twelve faces, often ending in **pyramids**, with three, six, or twelve triangular faces, meeting each other at a point. Trigonal minerals may also occur as six-sided **rhombohedra** with parallel pairs of rhombic faces.

Tetragonal minerals These are found as prismatic crystals with four or eight faces, ending in pyramids or bounded by a series of faces all lying at different angles to one another.

Orthorhombic, monoclinic and triclinic minerals These display progressively less symmetry and often consist of pairs of parallel faces combined with other forms. They are often tabular in habit, bounded by a single pair of parallel faces, separated from one another by a whole series of much smaller faces.

Habit Crystals can also vary in shape according to which set of crystal faces is predominant. Prismatic crystals can take on a pyramidal habit if the prism faces are poorly developed or they may become acicular or needle-like if the prism faces are very elongate.

Crystal aggregates Minerals often occur as aggregates, taking on a form of their own. Acicular crystals may occur as fibrous aggregates, radiating from a centre and often displaying rounded surfaces to the outside, or all lying parallel to one another. Other minerals occur as platy aggregates, often described as scaly. More commonly, minerals just occur as granular aggregates, lacking any special form or internal structure, which is then described as **massive**.

Cleavage Minerals often split apart along **cleavage-planes**, following planes of weak bonding in the crystal lattice. If the mineral splits very easily, forming a smooth surface, which glints in the light, the cleavage is perfect. Less than perfect cleavage is often described as good, distinct or poor. If cleavage occurs in several different directions, the mineral may break into cleavage fragments.

Fracture Where a mineral lacks any cleavage, it usually breaks along an irregular surface to form a **fracture**. Conchoidal fracture is the most distinctive, forming a curved or slightly undulating surface with arcuate ridges, rather like broken glass.

Colour and streak Minerals may be transparent, translucent or opaque. Minute amounts of trace elements often affect their colour, making it an unreliable guide to their identification. However, opaque minerals may be distinguished by their streak. By drawing the mineral across an unglazed plate of porcelain, known as a streak-plate, a powder is produced, often with a distinctive colour.

Lustre This describes how a mineral reflects the light, sometimes in an opalescent or iridescent fashion with a play of colours. Otherwise, it can be metallic, vitreous, resinous, greasy, waxy, pearly, silky or earthy, while its intensity may be adamantine, splendent, shining, glistening or dull.

Density and hardness Only a few minerals are especially heavy, as defined by their **specific gravity** (SG), which is measured in relation to water (SG = 1). More useful is a mineral's **hardness**, which measures its resistance to scratching on the ten-point Moh's scale, as defined by the following minerals: 1) Talc; 2) Gypsum; 3) Calcite; 4) Fluorspar; 5) Apatite; 6) Orthoclase; 7) Quartz; 8) Topaz; 9) Corundum; and 10) Diamond. A mineral's hardness (H) is best estimated by attempting to scratch its surface, using a finger-nail (hardness around 2.5), a copper coin or brass pin (hardness around 5), or a knife-blade of good quality steel (hardness around 6.5).

Gold *Au*

Symbol of power and wealth, gold is occasionally found sparingly in quartz veins. It typically occurs scattered throughout the rock as irregular grains and larger nuggets, sometimes taking on a spongy or dendritic form. Its golden-yellow colour, density of 19.3 if pure and hardness of only 2.5 are all distinctive. Its malleable nature distinguishes it from pyrite and chalcopyrite, which are harder and more brittle minerals, often known as 'fools' gold'. If gold-bearing rocks undergo weathering, the gold may become concentrated in residual soils, or it may be washed into streams to form the alluvial deposits known as placers, from which it can be recovered by panning.

Sulphur *S*

Well-formed crystals and massive encrustations of native sulphur deposited by sublimation from volcanic gases are typically produced around volcanic vents and hot springs. Other deposits occur along with gypsum in the cap-rock of salt-domes. Deep yellow in colour, sometimes tinged red or green, but occasionally brownish, and translucent with a resinous lustre, the crystals are typically tabular in habit, sometimes bounded by pyramids. The cleavage is poor, and the fracture uneven. Native sulphur is distinctly soft with a hardness of 1.5 to 2.5, and low in specific gravity (around 2.0). It burns with a pale blue flame, giving off acid fumes, and melts at 113°C.

Halite (Rock Salt) *NaCl* × 1.5

Halite occurs as evaporite deposits, often in the form of salt-domes, which intrude the overlying sediments as plug-like masses. As well as granular masses, cubic crystals of halite sometimes occur with hopper faces, each showing a central depression with a step-like form. Cleavage is perfect in three directions at right angles, parallel to the cubic faces. Colourless or white when pure, halite is more often brownish, but sometimes occurs in shades of yellow or red. Appearing transparent or translucent, it has a vitreous lustre. It is easily distinguished by its extreme softness (hardness is 2.5), presence of cubic crystals with perfect cleavage, and a salty taste when licked.

Fluorite (or Fluorspar) *CaF$_2$* × 0.75

This translucent mineral is widely distributed in mineral veins, where it occurs along with quartz, calcite and barytes. It usually occurs as well-formed cubic crystals, but less commonly as octahedra, showing perfect cleavage in four directions, oblique to the cubic faces. It varies greatly in colour. Usually purple or violet, it may be blue, green, yellow, pink, white, colourless, or sometimes even black. Its hardness is 4. It is best recognized by the presence of octahedral cleavages, forming triangular facets to the corners of cubic crystals. Blue John is the deep-purple banded variety from Derbyshire, used as an ornamental stone.

This bronzy or brassy yellow mineral with a metallic lustre is known as 'fools' gold'. Pyrite commonly occurs as cubic crystals with striated faces as shown above, but it also forms nodules and granular masses in many different sedimentary, igneous and metamorphic rocks. It has a greenish-black streak and its hardness is 6 or 6.5. It resembles chalcopyrite (copper pyrites $CuFeS_2$), from which it can be distinguished by its lighter colour, greater hardness and the lack of an iridescent tarnish. It is very like marcasite as the other polymorph of iron sulphide. Pyrite is very susceptible to weathering, often leaving a residue of brownish limonite.

Galena *PbS*   × 1

This leaden grey and very dense mineral is the most important ore of lead, often occurring in mineral veins along with quartz, calcite, dolomite, fluorite, and barytes. Typically occurring as cubic or octahedral crystals, it has perfect cleavage in three directions at right angles, so that it breaks apart into cubic cleavage-fragments. Galena has a bright metallic lustre on fresh surfaces, which tarnish easily, becoming dull on exposure to the air. It is easily recognized by its colour, metallic lustre, perfect cleavage in three directions, hardness of only 2.5, and high density (SG 7.5). It is shown here enclosed in quartz.

Sphalerite (or Black Jack or Zinc Blende) *ZnS* × 2

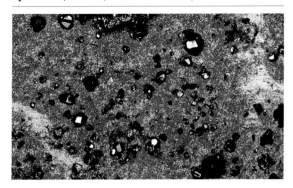

Occurring as the common ore of zinc, sphalerite is usually brown or black with a resinous lustre, but is sometimes reddish-brown or yellow and can be very pale or colourless. Its streak varies from reddish-brown to yellow or white. Crystals of the cubic system are common. They are often tetrahedral with four faces, or twelve-sided rhombic dodecahedra, and frequently distorted with curved faces. Sphalerite has perfect cleavage in six directions. It is also found as granular, fibrous and botryoidal masses. It can be hard to identify because of its variable colour, and its association with pyrite and galena in mineral veins, and its resinous lustre, are diagnostic.

Malachite and Azurite
$CuCO_3.Cu(OH)_2$ and $2CuCO_3.Cu(OH)_2$ × 1

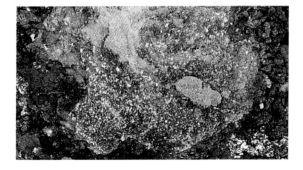

Malachite and azurite are hydrated carbonates of copper, typically formed by the weathering of copper deposits under oxidizing conditions close to the Earth's surface. Malachite is bright green, while azurite is deep azure blue. Malachite is monoclinic, but it is usually found as encrusting masses rather than crystals, typically forming a fibrous structure with a surface like a bunch of grapes. Azurite is orthorhombic, often occurring as tabular crystals or stubby prisms, rather than fibrous masses. Both minerals have a silky lustre if fibrous, but display a vitreous or adamantine lustre if well crystallized. Their hardness is 3.5 to 4.0, and the SG varies from 3.8 to 4.0.

Calcite is a common mineral, occurring in sedimentary limestones and metamorphic marbles, and often found in mineral veins. It forms stalactites and stalagmites in limestone caves, and deposits of travertine and tufa around hot springs. Crystals of the trigonal system are common and very varied in habit, while calcite also occurs as fibrous aggregates and granular masses. Cleavage is perfect in three directions at 75°, so that crystalline calcite tends to break into rhombohedral cleavage-fragments. Calcite is usually whitish in colour, but it can be colourless, or it may display shades of grey, green, yellow, red, blue and purple, or even brown or black.

Iceland Spar (Calcite) *CaCO₃*   × 1

If so pure that it is transparent, calcite is known as Iceland spar. It then breaks into perfect rhombohedral cleavage-fragments, which exhibit the optical phenomenon of double refraction. If an object like a coin (as shown here) is viewed through a rhomb of Iceland spar, it appears as two images. When the rhomb is rotated, one image remains stationary, while the other rotates around the fixed position of the first image. Double refraction is caused by the light splitting into two rays as it passes through the crystalline structure of the mineral, travelling at different velocities in slightly different directions.

Dog-tooth and Nail-head Spar (Calcite) $CaCO_3$

Dog-tooth spar is formed by calcite crystals with sharp terminations, each having six triangular faces known as scalenohedra lying at an acute angle to one another, giving the appearance of a dog's tooth. Nail-head spar consists of prismatic crystals of calcite with flat rhombohedral terminations, that look like the flat heads of cut nails, once used to secure floorboards. Whatever their form, calcite crystals usually display vitreous lustre, sometimes appearing pearly on their cleavage-planes. The hardness is 3, and defines this point on Moh's scale, so that calcite is easily scratched with a knife, while the SG is 2.7.

Above: *Dog-tooth Spar* × 0.25
Below: *Nail-head Spar* × 0.5

Aragonite $CaCO_3$

× 2

Aragonite occurs as the less stable form of calcium carbonate, forming a polymorph of calcite. Belonging to the orthorhombic system, it is often found as fibrous masses of acicular crystals. Prismatic crystals commonly display pseudo-hexagonal symmetry, as shown here, formed by the repeated twinning of the crystal structure across the prism faces, lying at 64° to one another. Aragonite is usually whitish in colour, but it may be tinged grey, yellow or brown. It typically occurs as an encrusting deposit around hot springs, while it is found associated with beds of gypsum. It also makes up the shells of present-day molluscs.

13

Dolomite $CaCO_3.MgCO_3$ × 2

Dolomite is very similar to calcite, lacking any distinctive features unless it occurs as rhombohedral crystals with curved faces, as shown here with haematite. Often found as a vein mineral, it is also the chief constituent of the rock known as dolomite. Ankerite is an iron-rich dolomite in which iron has substituted for magnesium in the crystal lattice, giving it a darker-brown colour. Siderite $FeCO_3$ is a common constituent of shales and mudstones, occurring as massive but very fine-grained concretions in clay-band ironstones. It can be distinguished from calcite and dolomite by its higher density (SG 3.8 to 4.0), greater hardness (3.5 to 4.5) and darker colour.

Rhodochrosite $MnCO_3$ × 2

Quite distinctive in displaying a rose-pink colour, rhodochrosite is otherwise much like calcite and dolomite. It is rarely found as well-formed crystals, occurring instead as granular masses with a banded structure, as shown here. Weathering to a brown or black crust if exposed to the air, it typically occurs as a vein mineral, often associated with silver, lead and copper ores. Magnesite $MgCO_3$ is a carbonate mineral which is difficult to distinguish from calcite and dolomite. It is usually found as an alteration product of magnesium-rich rocks like serpentine or dolomite, often occurring as granular or fibrous masses in the form of veins or more irregular bodies.

Gypsum $CaSO_4.H_2O$

Gypsum is the hydrated form of calcium sulphate, commonly found in evaporite deposits along with anhydrite and halite. Often occurring as granular or fibrous masses, any crystals are usually tabular in habit, sometimes with curved faces. Alabaster is very fine-grained and massive, while fibrous gypsum is known as satin spar. Cleavage is perfect in one direction, but much less distinct in two other directions. It is usually colourless or white, but may also occur in shades of yellow, grey, red and brown. Its hardness is 2 and it is easily scratched with a finger-nail. Shown here is daisy-bed gypsum with rosettes of fibrous crystals.

Selenite and Desert Roses (Gypsum) $CaSO_4.H_2O$

Selenite × 0.25

Below:
Desert Roses × 0.5

Selenite is found as colourless and transparent crystals of pure gypsum, which can be broken along the single direction of perfect cleavage into very thin, flexible plates, which can be cut. Desert roses are radiating masses of platy crystals consisting of gypsum, which are characteristic of sabkhas or salt-marshes in desert regions, where they are precipitated by the evaporation of ground-water.

Anhydrite $CaSO_4$

Anhydrite is the anhydrous form of calcium sulphate, which is commonly found in evaporite deposits, where it may be formed by the dehydration of gypsum. It only precipitates directly from the evaporation of seawater at temperatures over 42°C. Crystals are rare, but if present, they show three perfect cleavages at 90°. Anhydrite more usually occurs as granular or fibrous masses. It is usually white, often with a bluish tinge, but is sometimes grey or reddish, while crystals may be colourless and transparent. Lustre is vitreous, but pearly on cleavage-planes. It is best distinguished from calcite and gypsum by its higher density (SG 2.9), and greater hardness (3.0 to 3.5), respectively.

Barytes (or Barite) $BaSO_4$

Barytes is most commonly found as a vein mineral associated with galena and fluorite. Crystals with orthorhombic symmetry are common, often tabular or prismatic with diamond-shaped outlines. They have perfect cleavage in two directions at 78°, together with a third direction at 90° to the other two cleavages. Granular or fibrous masses also occur, sometimes appearing like a cockscomb. Barytes is usually white in colour, often tinged yellow, brown or red, but sometimes bluish or greenish; crystals may be colourless and transparent with a vitreous lustre, sometimes appearing resinous or pearly. It is easily distinguished by its unusually high density (SG 4.5) for such a pale-coloured mineral.

Apatite $Ca_5(PO_4)_3(F,Cl,OH)$ × 4

Apatite is not only found in igneous and metamorphic rocks, but it also makes up fossil bones, occurring as cryptocrystalline collophane. As well as granular masses, crystals are sometimes tabular but usually hexagonal prisms with pyramidal terminations, showing a poor cleavage in one direction with an uneven or conchoidal fracture. Transparent or translucent with a vitreous lustre, it is usually greenish or greyish-green, but sometimes white, brown, yellow, bluish or reddish, showing a white streak. The specific gravity is 3.2, while the hardness is 5, defining this point on Moh's scale, so it can be scratched with a knife unlike other hexagonal minerals like beryl.

Haematite Fe_2O_3

Haematite is the most important ore of iron. It typically occurs in two quite distinct forms. Kidney iron-ore is found in rounded masses which, if broken apart, display a fibrous structure with a silky sheen and a metallic lustre radiating from their centres. Specular iron-ore usually consists of tabular or rhombohedral crystals,

Above: *Kidney Iron-ore* × 0.33
Below: *Specular Iron-ore* × 0.33

sometimes with curved and striated faces, and displaying a metallic and very shiny lustre. The colour is steely-grey or iron-black, and the crystals are opaque, except when in very thin flakes. Diagnostic properties of haematite are its cherry-red streak, specific gravity of 4.9 to 5.3 and hardness of 5 to 6.

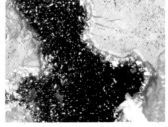

Magnetite Fe_3O_4

Magnetite is an extremely common but rarely abundant constituent of many igneous and metamorphic rocks. As well as granular masses, octahedral crystals are common but are usually very small, iron-black in colour, and often have a bluish tarnish. It has a black streak. Magnetite is strongly magnetic, unlike ilmentite $FeO.TiO_2$, which typically occurs as tabular or scaly crystals with a brownish-black streak. Spinel $MgO.Al_2O_3$ also resembles magnetite, occurring as octahedral crystals, but it is usually red and translucent rather than black and opaque, with a superior hardness (H 7.8 to 8.0). Chromite $FeO.Cr_2O_3$ is a chrome-rich variety with a dark brown streak, but is only weakly magnetic.

Rutile TiO_2 × 2

Rutile is a tetragonal form of titanium oxide. Crystals are common as elongate prisms with striated faces and bipyramidal terminations, which are often found making up knee-shaped twins. Cleavage is poor in two directions, with an uneven fracture. Rutile is usually reddish-brown in colour with an adamantine lustre, but it may be yellowish-red or black. The streak is pale brown. The specific gravity is 4.2 to 4.4, and the hardness 6.0 to 6.5. Occurring commonly in igneous and metamorphic rocks, but only in small amounts, it is also found as needle-like inclusions in other minerals like quartz and feldspar. It is often concentrated in beach sands and alluvial deposits.

Cassiterite SnO_2

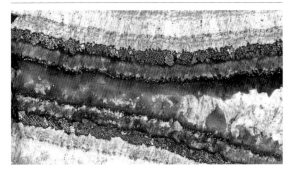

Cassiterite is the principal ore of tin, typically found in mineral and pegmatite veins associated with granites. Crystals of the tetragonal system are common, usually occurring as pseudo-octahedral bipyramids and stubby prisms, which form knee-shaped twins. Cleavage is poor in several directions, and the fracture uneven. Cassiterite also occurs in granular or fibrous masses. It is commonly reddish-brown or almost black in colour, but sometimes yellow, with an adamantine lustre, while the streak is white or grey. It is best identified from other dark minerals by its density (SG 6.8 to 7.1) and superior hardness (H 6 to 7), along with its pale streak, adamantine lustre and crystal form.

Corundum Al_2O_3

Corundum occurs only rarely, but it is important as a gemstone. Usually translucent unless of gem quality, crystals commonly occur as rough, barrel-shaped prisms with hexagonal cross-sections, ending in steep, six-sided pyramids, which are spindle-shaped if the prism faces are lacking. Granular masses form emery when mixed with magnetite and spinel. Displaying an adamantine or vitreous lustre, the crystals lack any cleavage. They vary greatly in colour, but corundum of gem quality occurs as blue sapphire and red ruby. It is best distinguished by crystal form and a hardness of 9, defining this point on the Moh's scale. Corundum is the hardest mineral after diamond.

Pyrolusite is most commonly observed wherever it makes the dark dendritic or branching patterns with a strange plant-like appearance on joints and bedding-planes. These form in response to the oxidation of manganese-bearing minerals in the surrounding rocks during near-surface weathering. Pyrolusite may also occur with psilomelane, the hydrated oxide of manganese, without any fixed composition, forming botryoidal masses like kidney iron-ore, from which it can best be distinguished by its darker colour and black streak.

Limonite (Goethite) $FeO(OH)$ Field of view 2m

Limonite is best used as a field term to describe all the hydrated oxides of iron, formed by the alteration of iron-bearing minerals in rocks undergoing weathering, and which are often found coating joints and bedding-planes with films of yellowish-brown material, as shown here. It is an important constituent of bog iron-ore, formed by the reducing action of bacteria in swampy conditions. Goethite is a crystalline form, although it is often very fine-grained and earthy. It is usually reddish- or yellowish-brown, but appears very dark brown with a yellowish-brown streak if crystalline. It may be confused with kidney iron-ore, but the streak is distinctive.

Quartz is very common in sedimentary, igneous and metamorphic rocks, and it is also often found in mineral veins. Crystals are rare except in these mineral veins and cavities, typically occurring as hexagonal prisms with pyramidal terminations, and often displaying striated faces. Quartz is more usually found as massive aggregates or is disseminated as grains throughout the rock. It is transparent or translucent, and often coloured milky-white in vein quartz, but otherwise it appears colourless or grey, or occasionally opalescent with a bluish tinge. It is best identified by its vitreous lustre, lack of cleavage and con-

choidal fracture, giving it a glassy appearance. Its hardness of 7 defines this point on Moh's scale.

Vein Quartz *SiO$_2$*

Quartz commonly occurs in mineral veins, either by itself or together with other minerals like calcite, dolomite and barytes. It may be found as well-formed crystals, especially where cavities are present, occupying the centre of the vein itself. Typically, the pyramidal terminations of the individual crystals project into these cavities. However, vein quartz more commonly occurs as milky quartz, often without any discernible crystals being present. Its milky-white colour is caused by a multitude of very small cavities, which refract the light, but it otherwise shares the same physical

Above: *Quartz Vein*
Below: *Vein Quartz* × 0.25

and chemical properties as the more translucent varieties of quartz.

21

Semi-precious Quartz SiO_2

Amethyst × 0.35

Smoky Quartz × 0.35

The following varieties of semi-precious quartz can be distinguished. Rock crystal is the purest and most transparent form, not necessarily occurring as well-formed crystals. Blue quartz displays a blue opalescent colour, developed by minute needles of rutile or tourmaline. Amethyst is coloured purple or violet by traces of manganese or ferric iron, perhaps in conjunction with natural radiation. Rose quartz is pale pink or rose-coloured, the colour caused by traces of manganese, titanium or lithium. Citrine is coloured yellow by traces of ferric hydroxide in a colloidal state. Smoky quartz or Cairngorm is a smoky yellow or darker brown colour, caused by traces of aluminium. Morion is a nearly black variety of smoky quartz.

Chalcedony SiO_2

Above: *Chrysoprase* × 0.75
Below: *Jasper* × 0.5

Chalcedony is a crypto-crystalline type of silica, formed by minute crystals of quartz with sub-microscopic pores, displaying a vitreous or a rather waxy lustre. Carnelian is translucent, coloured red or reddish-brown, chrysoprase is apple-green, while heliotrope is bright green, speckled with red. Chert and flint are opaque varieties of chalcedony, usually dull grey to black in colour, commonly found in sedimentary rocks. Jasper gets its red colour from the presence of finely disseminated iron oxides, although it is often just cryptocrystalline quartz, rather than chalcedony. Chalcedony differs from opal in its superior hardness (H 6.5) and higher density (SG 2.6).

Agate SiO_2

Agate is an ornamental variety of finely banded chalcedony, coloured by impurities like manganese and iron. Differing shades of white, milky-white and grey are usually present, but sometimes green, brown, red or black colours are developed, changing abruptly or shading off imperceptibly across the banding. It is typically deposited as a concentric lining in the gas-cavities of lava flows, and in other forms of hollow geode. Moss agate is a pale-coloured chalcedony displaying dendritic patterns in green, brown or black, owing to the presence of manganese oxide, while onyx is a form of agate in which the colour banding is straight and parallel.

Opal $SiO_2.nH_2O$ × 0.5

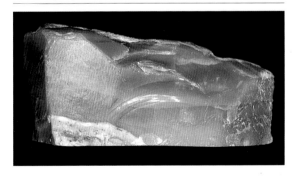

Opal is an amorphous or cryptocrystalline form of silica which contains a variable amount of water in sub-microscopic pores. Transparent to translucent, it is usually colourless or milky-white, and often opalescent with a bluish tinge, but occasionally coloured red, brown, green or even nearly black. It is usually massive, with a vitreous or resinous lustre, and a conchoidal fracture. If it exhibits a marked opalescence with a brilliant display of body colours, usually blues, reds and yellows, it can be used as a semi-precious stone. Opal is best distinguished from chalcedony by its lower density (SG 1.8 to 2.3) and its inferior hardness of 5.5 to 6.5.

Feldspars $KAlSi_3O_8$, $NaAlSi_3O_8$–$CaAl_2Si_2O_8$

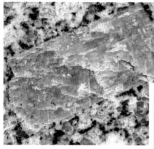

*Potash
Feldspar* × 1

Below:
Amazonstone × 0.35

Feldspars are the most abundant of all the rock-forming minerals, especially in igneous rocks. They occur as several different varieties, difficult to tell apart in hand specimen. Crystals are usually tabular, showing perfect cleavages in two directions at right angles, or nearly so. Translucent with a vitreous lustre, but appearing somewhat pearly on cleavage surfaces, feldspar varies in colour from white or grey to pink or red, while amazonstone is green. Its hardness is 6.0 to 6.5, slightly less than quartz. Feldspar often appears opaque and porcellaneous, owing to slight alteration, distinguishing it from 'glassy' quartz, which also lacks any cleavage.

Potash Feldspar $KAlSi_3O_8$ × 0.5

Potash feldspars are formed by orthoclase, sanidine and microcline, all sharing the same chemical composition, but differing slightly from one another in atomic structure and crystal form. Low-temperature orthoclase and microcline look very alike in the field, while high-temperature sanidine is colourless and rather transparent. Orthoclase displays simple twinning, seen wherever the two halves of a crystal reflect the light differently, while microcline displays 'cross-hatched' twinning, visible only under the microscope. Shown here is perthite, forming an intergrowth of microcline with sodic plagioclase, which separated out as the temperature fell after crystallization.

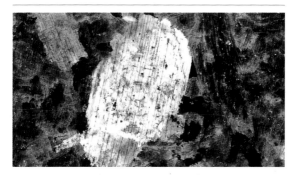

Plagioclase feldspar forms a continuous series of solid solutions, varying gradually in composition from sodic plagioclase or albite $NaAlSi_3O_8$ to calcic plagioclase or anorthite $CaAl_2Si_2O_8$ as calcium and aluminium substitute for sodium and silicon within the crystal lattice. The intermediate members of this series are known respectively as oligoclase, andesine, labradorite and bytownite, which become progressively more calcic and less sodic in passing from albite to anorthite. The plagioclase feldspars are nearly always twinned repeatedly within a single crystal, giving a striated appearance to the cleavage-planes, which can occasionally be seen in hand specimen. Plagioclase is nearly always white or grey in colour.

Nepheline $NaAlSiO_4$ × 1.5

Nepheline is a feldspathoid mineral, occurring as the silica-deficient equivalent of sodic plagioclase. Such minerals are only found in igneous rocks without any free quartz, since they would otherwise combine with silica to form feldspar. Crystals form stumpy hexagonal prisms, ending in a pair of flat faces, with poor cleavage in several different directions, and a conchoidal fracture. Transparent or translucent, nepheline is typically colourless, white, grey or pink. It is often difficult to distinguish from quartz and feldspar, apart from its greasy lustre, inferior hardness of 5 to 6 and its crystal form. It is typically found in alkaline igneous rocks such as nepheline-syenites and phonolites.

Leucite $KAlSi_2O_6$

Leucite is a common feldspathoid mineral, typically found only in potash-rich lavas as the silica-deficient equivalent of potash feldspar. Crystals are trapezohedrons, each with twenty-four faces, giving them a rounded form. They show conchoidal fracture along with imperfect cleavages in several different directions, often displaying a vitreous lustre on fractured surfaces. Leucite is translucent or opaque and typically white or ash-grey. Its hardness is 5.5 to 6.0, and the specific gravity 2.5. It is difficult to distinguish from analcite in hand specimen, except that leucite typically occurs as phenocrysts within lava flows, while analcite is usually found as a secondary mineral in volcanic vesicles and similar cavities.

Analcite (or Analcime) $NaAlSi_2O_6.H_2O$ × 2

Although resembling the feldspathoids, analcite is usually classified as a zeolite mineral belonging to a complex group of hydrated sodium, potassium or calcium alumino-silicate minerals. They typically occur as secondary minerals in the vesicles of basaltic lava flows, or sometimes in hydrothermal veins cutting across such rocks. If well-crystallized, analcite occurs as trapezohedrons with twenty-four faces, displaying a poor cleavage and an uneven fracture with a vitreous lustre. Transparent or translucent, it is usually colourless, white or grey, but is sometimes tinged with yellow, pink, red or green. With a hardness of 5.5, it is difficult to distinguish from leucite, apart from its mode of occurrence.

Prehnite $Ca_2Al_2Si_3O_{10}(OH)_2$

Prehnite is a hydrated alumino-silicate of calcium, usually found associated with zeolites such as analcite, and often filling veins and cavities in lava flows. Well-formed crystals with a single direction of cleavage are rare, since prehnite usually occurs as rounded masses with a fibrous structure. Transparent or translucent, it is usually a pale watery green in colour, but otherwise white, yellow or grey. It has a vitreous lustre and an uneven fracture. Its hardness of 6.0 to 6.5 and specific gravity of 2.9 to 3.0 are much greater than in associated minerals such as zeolites. Prehnite is best recognized by its distinctive green colour and rounded habit, along with its mode of occurrence.

Talc (Steatite) $Mg_3Si_4O_{10}(OH)_2$

Talc or steatite is a hydrated silicate of magnesium, similar in composition to serpentine but differing slightly in its atomic proportions, and formed by the alteration of ultrabasic rocks. Crystals are rarely well developed, occurring instead as foliated or granular masses. Cleavage is perfect in one direction. Translucent to the light, talc is white, grey or pale green in colour, but is often stained red. It has a pearly lustre with a greasy or even soapy feel. Massive varieties are known as steatite or soapstone. Its hardness defines the lowest point on Moh's scale. It is best recognized by its extreme softness, being easily scratched with a finger-nail, and its greasy or soapy feel.

Muscovite $KAl_2(AlSi_3O_{10})(OH,F)_2$

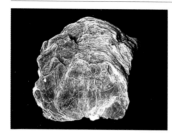

Above: *Muscovite* × 0.75
Below: *Lepidolite* × 0.75

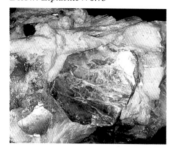

Muscovite is the common variety of white mica found in granites and granite-pegmatites and in schists. It is often almost colourless with a pearly lustre and splits readily into very thin flexible sheets along a perfect basal cleavage. Crystals are tabular or platy with pseudo-hexagonal outlines, but they can also occur in scaly masses and in disseminated flakes. Sericite is a very finely divided muscovite found as an alteration product, especially of feldspars, resulting from hydrothermal activity or weathering. Lepidolite is a lithium mica which differs from ordinary muscovite in its pale lilac colour. It is found most commonly in granite pegmatites.

Biotite $K(MgFe)_3AlSi_3O_{10}(OH,F)_2$ × 1.5

Biotite is the iron-rich mica, easily distinguished from muscovite by its dark brown, greenish-brown or black colour, commonly found in igneous and metamorphic rocks, particularly granites and schists. Phlogopite is a magnesia-rich variety of biotite, distinguished by its paler colour, which varies from a translucent yellow to a more opaque reddish-brown, often with a coppery tinge. It is found in metamorphosed dolomitic limestones, as well as in ultrabasic igneous rocks. Chlorites resemble biotite and phlogopite in that they are hydrated alumino-silicates of iron and magnesium, but they lack any potassium. They typically occur as very fine-grained alteration products and often have a very distinctive greenish colour.

Hornblende, commonly found in igneous and metamorphic rocks, belongs to a complex group of hydrous alumino-silicates rich in magnesium, iron and calcium (or sodium) called the amphiboles. These all have two cleavages roughly at 120° to one another, which distinguish them from pyroxenes such as augite. Crystals typically occur as six-sided prisms, often rather elongate with flattened cross-sections. Fibrous, acicular or granular masses are also found. Hornblende is usually opaque or nearly so, with a vitreous lustre. The colour is often nearly black, sometimes tinged with brown, but dark or more rarely light green, and dark brown varieties also occur. The specific gravity is 3.0 to 3.5 and the hardness 5 to 6.

Tremolite and Actinolite *Ca$_2$(Mg,Fe)$_5$(Si$_4$O$_{11}$)(OH)$_2$*

Tremolite × 0.33

Below:
Actinolite × 0.67

Tremolite and actinolite are found in metamorphosed limestones, dolomites and basic igneous rocks. Crystals typically occur as blade-like or very elongate prisms, sometimes forming acicular, fibrous or felted masses. Tremolite is transparent or translucent, and typically white or grey, while actinolite is light to dark green. The specific gravity varies from 3.0 to 3.4 according to iron content. Tremolite is the more magnesium-rich variety, typical of thermally metamorphosed limestones and dolomites with a higher than usual content of silica; actinolite is the darker and more iron-rich variety, more often found in metamorphosed igneous rocks of a basic composition.

29

Commonly found in igneous and metamorphic rocks, augite belongs to a complex group of anhydrous alumino-silicates, principally of magnesium, iron and calcium, sometimes combined with sodium, known as pyroxenes. Unlike the amphiboles, which they otherwise resemble, they all have two directions of cleavage roughly at right angles to one another. Crystals typically occur as stout prisms, square or octagonal in cross-section. Augite is usually almost black in colour, but is sometimes greenish-black, with a vitreous lustre. The specific gravity is 3.2 to 3.6, increasing with iron content, and the hardness 5.5 to 6.5. Augite is widely distributed in basic and ultrabasic igneous rocks such as basalt, dolerite, gabbro and peridotite.

Diopside *CaMg(Si$_2$O$_6$)*

Above: *Diopside* × 0.75
Below: *Diallage* × 0.75

Diopside is a pyroxene that is closely related to augite in its chemical composition and crystal structure, but it is typically found in impure limestones affected by contact or regional metamorphism, along with basic and ultrabasic igneous rocks. It usually occurs in granular masses. It can best be distinguished from augite by its pale dirty green or even whitish colour, reflecting a lack of iron in its chemical composition. Diallage is a translucent variety of augite or diopside which has a metallic or bronzy lustre, best seen when the crystals reflect the light in a certain direction.

$Olivine\ (Mg,Fe)_2SiO_4$

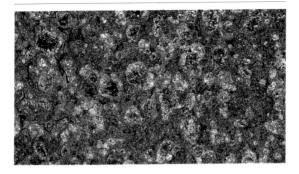

Olivine is a silicate of iron and magnesium commonly found in basic and ultrabasic igneous rocks. It occurs less commonly as magnesia-rich fosterite in metamorphosed siliceous dolomites. Crystals are rarely well developed as short prisms with pointed terminations, since this mineral usually occurs as discrete grains and granular masses. Cleavage is very poor with a conchoidal fracture. If unaltered, it is typically olive-green in colour, and transparent or translucent, but it becomes darker and more opaque as the iron content increases. The specific gravity is 3.2 to 4.4, increasing with iron content, and the hardness 6 to 7. It is often altered by hydrothermal activity into serpentine and magnetite.

Serpentine $Mg_3Si_2O_5(OH)_4$

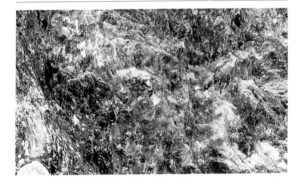

Serpentine is commonly found in basic and ultrabasic igneous rocks as an alteration product of magnesium-rich minerals like olivine and orthopyroxene, forming hydrated alumino-silicates of magnesium. Crystals are rarely well developed, since this mineral commonly occurs as fibrous chrysotile, or platy antigorite, along with more massive and fine-grained varieties, often displaying a conchoidal or splintery fracture. It is translucent or opaque, usually green in colour, varying in shade to almost black, while it may be stained red, yellow or brown. It has a distinctive waxy lustre with a greasy feel, but silky if fibrous, or earthy if massive. Its hardness varies from 2.5 to 4.0.

Epidote and zoisite belong to a complex group of slightly hydrous silicate minerals, principally of aluminium and calcium (zoisite), together with iron (epidote) and manganese (piedmontite). Crystals are typically prismatic, often elongated, with striated faces, but often form granular, acicular or fibrous masses. Cleavage is perfect in one direction, with a pearly lustre. The colour is typically a dirty pistachio-green in epidote, but shades of grey, yellow, brown and black also occur, as well as rose-pink (thulite) and reddish-brown (piedmontite). The specific gravity is 3.2 to 3.4, and the hardness 6 to 7. Epidote typically occurs as an alteration product in low-grade metamorphic rocks, sometimes forming in hydrothermal veins.

Tourmaline $Na(Mg,Fe,Li,Al,Mn)_3Al_6(BO_3)_3Si_6O_{18}(OH,F)_4$ × 1

Tourmaline is an extremely complex hydrous alumino-silicate, principally of sodium, magnesium, iron and boron, together with lithium, manganese and fluorine, which is often found as large crystals in granite pegmatites and altered granites. Crystals typically occur as elongate prisms with triangular cross-sections and curved and striated faces, ending in blunt three-sided pyramids, often found in radiating masses. Most varieties are opaque or nearly so with a vitreous lustre. Tourmaline is usually black or bluish-black, very rarely colourless and transparent, but shades of blue, green or red are occasionally found. The specific gravity is 3.0 to 3.2, and the hardness 7. The lack of a good cleavage serves to distinguish it from hornblende.

Beryl $Be_3Al_2Si_6O_{18}$

Beryl is widely distributed in granite pegmatites, occurring very rarely as gigantic crystals up to 9m in length and weighing over 25 tonnes. Crystals are common as hexagonal prisms, often having striated faces and blunt terminations, with only a single cleavage of poor quality and a conchoidal fracture. Beryl is transparent or translucent with a vitreous lustre and it is often a distinctive green colour, but it may be blue, yellow, pink, or white. The specific gravity is 2.6 to 2.8 and the hardness is 7.5 to 8.0, making beryl harder than apatite (and quartz), which it otherwise resembles. Transparent crystals of good quality give emeralds (green) or aquamarine (pale blue) as gemstones.

Topaz $Al_2SiO_4(OH,F)_2$

Topaz is a hydrous silicate of aluminium and fluorine, commonly found in granite pegmatites along with fluorite, cassiterite, tourmaline, beryl and apatite. The well-developed crystals often have many faces, consisting mostly of prismatic and pyramidal forms, with a single direction of perfect cleavage. Topaz is transparent or translucent with a vitreous lustre, and often of gem quality; it is usually colourless, but is sometimes pale yellow, pale blue, greenish, or more rarely pink. The specific gravity is 3.5 to 3.6, while the hardness is 8, defining this point on Moh's scale. It differs from other exceptionally hard minerals like beryl and corundum in its crystal form and perfect cleavage.

The distinctive garnet is found in metamorphic rocks like schists and amphibolites. Crystals commonly occur as twelve-sided rhombododecahedra or as icositetrahedra with twenty-four faces, lacking any cleavage. The specific gravity is 3.6 to 4.3, depending on variety, and the hardness 6.0 to 7.5. The following transparent or translucent varieties with a vitreous or resinous lustre can be recognized: Mg-rich Pyrope (blood-red, and often very dark); Fe-rich almandine (red, brownish-red or black); Mn-rich spessartine (dark red, brown or orange-yellow); Ca-rich grossular (green or yellowish-brown); Ca and Fe-rich andradite (yellow, green, brown or black); and Cr-rich uvarovite (a clear green). Garnet is often altered to greenish chlorite.

Staurolite *(Fe,Mg)$_2$(Al,Fe)$_9$Si$_4$O$_{20}$(O,OH)$_2$* × 1

Staurolite is a hydrous alumino-silicate of iron and magnesium, which occurs with garnet and kyanite in metamorphic schists and gneisses. Crystals are common as large porphyroblasts, set in a finer-grained groundmass, and often displaying a dull, rough surface. They are usually prismatic with blunt terminations, often occurring as cross-shaped twins, with a distinct cleavage in one direction. Staurolite is translucent or nearly opaque with a vitreous or resinous lustre. It is typically reddish-brown or brownish-black, rarely yellowish-brown. The specific gravity is 3.7 to 3.8, and the hardness 7.0 to 7.5. Its brownish colour, crystal form and occurrence as porphyroblasts in metamorphic rocks are characteristic.

Cordierite is an alumino-silicate of magnesium and iron, typically present with andalusite in metamorphic rocks formed from alumina-rich mudstones and shales. Usually found in discrete grains or granular masses, crystals occur rarely as short six-sided prisms. Transparent or translucent with vitreous lustre, cordierite is greyish-blue, lilac-blue or darker blue. The specific gravity is 2.5 to 2.8, increasing with iron content, and the hardness 7.0 to 7.5. If present as colourless grains in thermally metamorphosed rocks, cordierite is often very difficult to distinguish from quartz. It alters to a fine-grained aggregate of chlorite and muscovite, known as pinnite, weathering out to give a pitted surface to the rock.

Andalusite *Al₂SiO₅* × 0.5

Andalusite is a polymorph of kyanite and sillimanite, only differing from these minerals in crystal structure. Crystals are common as porphyroblasts in metamorphic rocks, and are usually prismatic with nearly square cross-sections, showing a poor cleavage in two directions at right angles. Transparent or nearly opaque with a vitreous lustre, but often cloudy with inclusions, andalusite is commonly pink, white or red, but sometimes pearly grey, violet, yellow or green. The specific gravity is 3.1 to 3.2, and the hardness 6.5 to 7.5. Chiastolite is a variety of andalusite with carbonaceous inclusions, arranged to form a dark cross, dividing up the square cross-sections of the crystals into a series of triangular segments.

35

Kyanite has the same chemical composition as andalusite and sillimanite, only differing from these minerals in crystal structure. It is most commonly found in regionally metamorphosed rocks like schists and gneisses. Crystals are common, usually forming elongate prisms with a flat, blade-like habit, showing cleavage in two directions nearly at right angles. Transparent or translucent with a vitreous lustre, appearing pearly on cleavage faces, the crystals are typically a light blue, often darker towards their centres, but sometimes white, grey, green, pink or even black. The specific gravity is 3.5 to 3.6, while the hardness is 6 to 7 along the length of the crystals, but only 4 to 5 crosswise.

Sillimanite Al_2SiO_5 × 2

Sillimanite is yet another polymorph of andalusite and kyanite, formed at higher temperatures and pressures than andalusite, but under lower pressures than kyanite. It is present in high-grade schists and gneisses. The long needle-like crystals with a prismatic habit and a perfect cleavage often appear fibrous, as in fibrolite, while they usually occur as felted masses. Transparent or translucent with a vitreous lustre and a silky sheen, sillimanite is usually white or pale grey, but sometimes yellowish, brown or greyish-green. The specific gravity is 3.3, and the hardness 6.5 to 7.5. Its recognition is difficult in hand specimen, particularly where it occurs as very small needles in the groundmass of metamorphic rocks.

Sedimentary rocks are deposited at the Earth's surface from waste material, consisting mostly of mineral grains and rock fragments derived from the weathering and erosion of pre-existing rocks. This **sedimentary detritus** is carried away from its source under the influence of gravity, often by running water but also by other agencies, such as the wind and glaciers, until it is eventually deposited as flat-lying layers of **detrital sediment**, usually but not always on the sea floor.

As deposition continues, this sediment is then buried under an ever-increasing load of overlying material. This causes **compaction** of the loose sediment, as water is gradually expelled from the pore spaces between the sedimentary grains. This is often accompanied by **cementation**, caused by mineral matter being deposited in the pore-spaces between these sedimentary grains, forming a cement. Acting together, these two processes convert the sedimentary material into a solid rock.

Equally, the remains of plants and animals may accumulate as **organic deposits** after their death, while the evaporation of sea water allows **chemical deposits** to form by precipitation, so forming the other two categories of sedimentary rock.

Sedimentary strata exposed in canyon walls, Goosenecks State Park, Utah, USA.

Bedding or stratification Sedimentary rocks are nearly always deposited in the form of **sedimentary beds**, as the widespread layers making up a sedimentary sequence are known. Although individual beds are rarely more than half a metre thick, great thicknesses of sedimentary strata often accumulate over geological time. Since they are usually laid down horizontally on top of one another rather like a pack of cards, the oldest beds within any sequence occur at its base, passing upwards into ever-younger rocks. The layers can also be dated geologically according to the **geological time-scale** or **stratigraphic column** by studying the fossils preserved within each sedimentary sequence.

Conglomerates and breccias How sedimentary rocks are formed by the weathering and erosion of pre-existing rocks is clearly seen in the case of conglomerates and breccias. These rocks are just accumulations of rock fragments, greater than 2mm across, which can only have been derived from the physical breakdown of older rocks. **Conglomerates** consist of well-rounded pebbles and boulders, which were transported for some distance from their source to judge by their shape. **Breccias** consist of more angular fragments, derived from a nearby source.

Shales and mudstones Weathering and erosion may also reduce the rocks exposed on land into much smaller particles, providing another source of sedimentary material. If chemical weathering occurs, the minerals in these rocks are altered into clay particles, microscopic in size, although quartz and other more resistant minerals are not affected. Carried away by running water, clay particles can be transported far and wide until they eventually settle out of suspension in still water, often as mud on the sea floor, which eventually hardens into shale and mudstone. **Shales** are very fine-grained rocks composed of clay minerals, which split easily along the bedding plane, while **mudstones** are less fissile.

Sandstones, arkoses and greywackes The mineral grains which escape the effects of chemical weathering can also be transported away from their source. Such detritus is much coarser-grained than clay or mud, consisting mostly of sand, varying between $\frac{1}{16}$mm to 2mm in size. After its deposition, it becomes compacted and cemented together by mineral matter to form a solid rock. **Sandstones** typically consist of quartz, which is very resistant to chemical weathering. **Arkoses** are rich in feldspar as well as quartz, and are formed by the physical breakdown of granite and gneiss under arid conditions of very rapid erosion. **Greywackes** are impure sandstones consisting of a wide variety of rock fragments and mineral grains, set in a finer-grained matrix, rich in clay minerals. **Orthoquartzites** are quartz-rich sandstones in which quartz forms the cement between the quartz grains, typically forming a hard and splintery rock.

Limestones, dolomites and evaporites The chemical weathering of pre-existing rocks also produces material in solution, which eventually finds its way into the oceans, where it forms salt water by evaporation. The salts dissolved in sea water can be precipitated directly by further evaporation, so forming the salt deposits, or **evaporites**. They can also be abstracted by animals to form their shells, which may then accumulate as sedimentary deposits on the sea floor after their death. **Limestones** are formed partly as chemical precipitates and partly as accumulations of organic remains. They are calcareous rocks rich in calcite and, not surprisingly, they often have fossils preserved within them. Once deposited, limestones may be altered chemically by brines rich in dissolved salts to form **dolomite**. Finally, **coal deposits** are formed wherever plant remains accumulate under swampy conditions, which prevent the carbonaceous material from breaking down.

Conglomerates

Conglomerates are composed of pebbles (2 to 8mm), cobbles (8 to 264mm), and even larger boulders of pre-existing rocks, set in a finer-grained matrix of sedimentary material. They were formed by weathering and erosion of older rocks, from which these fragments were derived. They are typically water-worn with rounded outlines, testifying to the abrasion that occurred as they were carried from their source. Although conglomerates are now often found as beach deposits, formed by wave action, most conglomerates in the geological record were deposited by fast-flowing rivers. These issue from the foot of mountains undergoing rapid uplift and erosion to form alluvial fans and braided rivers.

Quartz Conglomerate

Quartz conglomerates are formed by rock fragments such as vein quartz, jasper, chert, flint and quartzite, which are especially resistant to chemical weathering. Such fragments are typically preserved during the long-continued transport of sedimentary detritus, which often results in the complete destruction of other chemically less stable rock types derived from their source area. They may even be derived from the weathering and erosion of older conglomerates containing quartz-rich pebbles. The rock fragments are usually well rounded, often occurring as quite small pebbles. Although now obsolete, puddingstone was an early name for such a quartz conglomerate, given because the pebbles looked like raisins or plums in a pudding.

Conglomerates containing pebbles or boulders formed by many different rock types are sometimes described as polygenetic. Indeed, they provide us with a sample of the rocks undergoing denudation in response to uplift and erosion within their source area. They may be formed by virtually any rock type but, as shown here, they often consist of coarse-grained rocks like granite and gneiss, or finer-grained volcanic rocks such as basalt and andesite, along with quartzite. They often make large boulders with less than perfect rounding. Most likely, these conglomerates were formed by rapid deposition at the foot of nearby mountains undergoing intense denudation as the result of equally rapid uplift.

Limestone Conglomerate

Conglomerates containing boulders and pebbles of limestone (or dolomite) occur only locally, close to their source, because long-continued transport by water would inevitably lead to their destruction. Typically, they are found interbedded with red sandstones, deposited under arid conditions. The source of the limestone fragments can often be identified wherever it is exposed locally as an outcrop of older rocks. These older rocks, originally exposed as uplands, were then attacked by weathering and erosion, and the fragments of limestone so produced were carried away to be deposited on the lower ground around their flanks. More commonly, such deposits form breccias rather than conglomerates (*see* Brockram, page 43).

Basal Conglomerate

The origin of conglomerates by the weathering and erosion of older rocks is graphically displayed wherever they are found lying on top of a surface of unconformity, which itself marks a structural break between older and younger rocks. The rocks lying below such an unconformity represent a terrain of older rocks, which acted as the source from which the pebbles and boulders were derived, while the conglomerate itself often occurs at the base of an overlying sequence of sedimentary rocks. Shown here is a conglomerate consisting of large boulders of quartzite and other rocks, resting with an abrupt break on top of an older sequence of steeply dipping slates.

Fluvio-glacial Sand and Gravel

Fluvio-glacial sands and gravels are deposited by streams of melt-water which issue from glaciers and larger ice sheets. Such deposits are now found in glaciated areas, dating from the very end of the Pleistocene Ice Age around 10,000 years ago, when the ice finally retreated. They are commonly deposited as river gravels and out-wash fans around the flanks of glaciated uplands, and may also be deposited by glacial streams, flowing through or underneath the ice, or across its surface. The pebbles, cobbles and larger boulders of such deposits are often surprisingly well rounded, suggesting that they were subjected to much abrasion during their transport. They are often interbedded with finer-grained sands, silts and clays.

Breccias

Breccias differ from conglomerates in that they consist of a jumble of angular rock fragments, set in a matrix of finer-grained material. The name comes from the Italian (*breccia*, rubble). The angular nature of the rock fragments can only mean that they were derived from a local source. Although most breccias are sedimentary in origin, typically occurring as scree deposits, they can also be formed by the *in situ* breakup of pre-existing rocks. Fault-breccias are produced by the fracturing of wall-rocks lying along a fault-plane, which is caused by fault movements. Volcanic breccias result from volcanic explosions breaking up solid rocks into angular fragments to form intrusion or explosion breccias, vent breccias and volcanic agglomerates.

Buried Landscapes

Breccias are often found banked as scree deposits against older rocks, which form what can only be described as a buried landscape. The picture shows coarse breccias lying close to the base of the Torridonian sandstone in the Northwest Highlands of Scotland, which were deposited about 1000 million years ago. They are banked to the right against Lewisian gneiss, which was metamorphosed at great depths around 2700 million years ago and brought to the surface by uplift and erosion over a long period. The contact between the breccia and the gneiss is steeply inclined, marking an ancient hillside of Lewisian gneiss. The fragments in the breccia are derived from the gneiss.

Brockram

Breccias consisting of angular fragments of Carboniferous limestone, set in a sandy matrix with well-rounded grains of millet-seed quartz, are known locally in the north of England as brockrams. Permo-Triassic in age, they were deposited under desert conditions as screes and alluvial fans. They occur locally to the west of the Pennines, then undergoing rapid uplift to expose the Carboniferous limestone. The fragments of grey limestone with occasional fossils are often dolomitized, becoming reddish or purple in colour. Similar rocks occur as the Dolomitic Conglomerate around Bristol, and further west in the Vale of Glamorgan, although the rock is really a breccia with angular fragments of dolomitized limestone.

Mud-flake Breccia

While most breccias are formed by fragments derived by the denudation of rocks lying beyond the area of their subsequent deposition, this is not always the case. Mud-flake breccias in particular are produced wherever muddy sediment dries out and breaks up into wafer-like fragments soon after its deposition. The fragments are then incorporated into an overlying bed of coarser-grained sandstone when it is deposited, so forming a mud-flake breccia. They can also be formed by the slumping of poorly consolidated sediments to form slump-breccias. Such deposits are sometimes known as penecontemporaneous or intraformational breccias to distinguish them from extraformational breccias (or conglomerates), consisting of fragments derived from an external source.

Boulder Clay and Tillite

A widespread and very distinctive deposit laid down underneath an ice sheet as it melts, boulder clay consists of rock fragments set in a matrix of stiff, fine-grained clay, lacking any stratification. The boulders, pebbles and even smaller fragments are usually rather angular, often with striated surfaces formed by abrasion as they were dragged across the underlying rock by the glacier. It is sometimes known as a till, which is an old Scottish word for a stiff clay with scattered boulders, often giving rather infertile and poorly drained ground. If lithified to form a solid rock, boulder clay forms a tillite, occasionally found as boulder beds, interbedded with other sedimentary rocks.

Melanges and Olistostromes

Boulder beds consisting of chaotic assemblages of broken-up and contorted rocks, varying greatly in rock type from one another, and often forming extremely large masses, are usually known as melanges or olistostromes. The fragments are commonly set in a shaly matrix, which is often highly sheared. They are often thought to be tectonic breccias, formed by earth movements, or submarine slide-deposits, as suggested by the name (Greek: *olistomai*, to slide), although their field-relations are usually very obscure. The Gwna Melange in North Wales occurs as an olistostrome with huge blocks of pale-coloured quartzite, lying in a finer-grained matrix of much darker rock, which was probably laid down as a submarine slide-deposit.

Sandstones

Sandstones are formed by sand grains, varying in diameter between ¼₆mm and 2mm. These grains are most usually quartz, occurring as fresh grains without any cleavage, and often greyish in colour with a slightly frosted surface, rather like water-worn fragments of clear glass. Other mineral grains such as feldspar and mica may be present together with fragments of fine-grained rocks. Feldspar can best be distinguished from quartz by its rather turbid appearance, often whitish or tinged pink, and the presence of a cleavage. Sandstones typically have a granular texture. They often weather to form a slightly rough surface rather like fine sandpaper, which is quite distinctive, as shown here.

Cross-bedded Sandstone

Sandstones often display cross-bedding, which occurs wherever there are internal bedding-planes lying at an angle to the bedding. These inclined bedding-planes define what are called the foreset beds. Cross-bedding results from the downstream migration of sand-bars as the bed was deposited. The flowing water sweeps the sand grains over the crests of the sand-bars so that they are deposited on their lee-slopes. Accumulating as foreset beds, they dip downstream at around 30°. The foreset beds are often curved so that they meet one another tangentially along their lower contacts, while they are typically truncated by erosion along their upper surfaces, as seen in this example.

45

Dune-bedded and Millet-seed Sandstone

Above: *Dune Bedding*
Below: *Millet-seed Sandstone* × 3

Wind-lain or aeolian sandstones from deserts often display cross-bedding on a large scale. It is called dune-bedding and it is formed by sand dunes migrating downwind as sand blows over their crests to cascade down their lee slopes under gravity. If deposition takes place at the same time, the sand accumulates as foreset beds, dipping at angles of about 33° to the horizontal, and stacked as sets on top of one another. Dune-bedded sandstones are often red in colour (*see* Ferruginous Sandstone, page 48), and are formed by extremely well-rounded sand grains with frosted surfaces, typical of millet-seed sandstone.

Graded Sandstone

Graded bedding is characteristic of some sandstones, such as greywackes, which become finer-grained towards the top of each bed, so that the coarsest particles occur at its base, as shown here. It is most likely produced by deposition from turbidity currents. Such turbulent suspensions of muddy sediment are able to flow down-slope across the sea floor by virtue of their greater density, triggered perhaps by slumping or earthquake shocks. As the turbidity current comes to rest, the largest and heaviest particles are deposited first, forming the base of the sedimentary bed, followed by ever smaller and lighter grains towards its top.

Sandstones vary in composition according to what rocks were exposed to weathering and erosion in their source area, as influenced by the prevailing climate. Quartz is most resistant to chemical breakdown, followed in order of decreasing stability by muscovite, microcline, orthoclase, plagioclase, hornblende, biotite, pyroxene and olivine. Accordingly, quartz is most commonly found in what are known as mature sandstones, often to the virtual exclusion of any other mineral. These are typically deposited in the shallow seas forming the continental shelves, far away from their source, after undergoing much reworking by waves and tidal currents. Such sandstones often have quartz as a cement (*see* Orthoquartzite, page 50).

Pebbly Sandstone and Grit × 4.4

Pebbly sandstone is a coarse-grained sandstone in which up to 20% of the detrital grains occur as pebbles exceeding 2mm in size. It becomes a conglomerate if such pebbles make up more than 20% of the rock. If the detrital grains are rather angular and poorly sorted, meaning that they vary in size, the rock was once known as a grit. Typically, it was a coarse-grained sandstone or a fine-grained conglomerate with a gritty texture, often deposited by rivers flowing across flood plains. The name is now obsolete except as a field-name, but it has passed into stratigraphic usage in referring to the Millstone Grit of northern England.

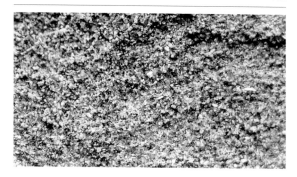

The appearance of a sandstone often depends on what minerals were deposited in its pore-spaces, forming the cement which holds the detrital grains together to form a solid rock. When first deposited, sandstones often have little sedimentary material lying between their grains, although clay minerals and very fine-grained carbonate mud may be present. Consolidation and lithification proceed as mineral matter is deposited in the pore-spaces around the grains, so reducing the porosity of the rock. Calcareous sandstones have calcite as a cement, often making the weathered rock appear pale in colour. Other pale-coloured sandstones may be cemented by dolomite, gypsum or barytes.

Ferruginous Sandstone × 1

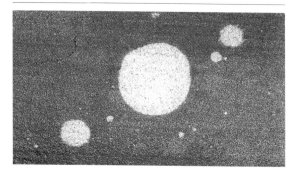

Ferruginous sandstones are coloured red, yellow or brown by iron oxides like haematite and limonite. Haematite usually just occurs as a thin coating on the grains, giving the rock a red colour, said to be typical of sandstones deposited under semi-arid conditions, especially in desert regions. It usually forms under oxidizing conditions, turning green on reduction to the ferrous form, as occurs in mottled sandstones with reduction spots, most likely formed around pyrite grains and carbonaceous fragments. Limonite as a hydrated oxide of ferrous iron is more commonly found in yellow or brownish sandstones. It is often formed by the near-surface weathering of haematite and other iron-rich minerals.

Micaceous sandstones typically contain detrital grains of muscovite, visible as glistening cleavage-flakes of silvery-grey muscovite on the bedding-planes. It often renders the rock fissile, allowing it to be split easily along the bedding, forming a flagstone. Detrital mica is typical of water-lain sandstones, often suggesting an alluvial origin. It is deposited by rivers flowing across their flood plains. It is most likely derived from the weathering and erosion of granite pegmatites, which often contain coarse-grained muscovite, although other source-rocks may include granite, gneiss and mica-schist. Biotite is much less common in micaceous sandstones, simply because it is more susceptible than muscovite to chemical breakdown.

Greensands

Greensands are marine sandstones, often rather calcareous in nature, which contain the green mineral glauconite. It is a hydrous alumino-silicate of potassium and iron, resembling micas and clay minerals in its crystal structure. It is found almost exclusively in marine sediments that were deposited rather slowly, especially where decaying organic matter is present in well-oxygenated waters. It typically occurs as very small, rounded grains with a dull lustre, often imparting a markedly green colour to the rocks if abundant, as in the Cretaceous greensands of southern England and the eastern USA. Glauconite-bearing rocks often weather yellow or brown, owing to the presence of limonite and other hydrated oxides of iron.

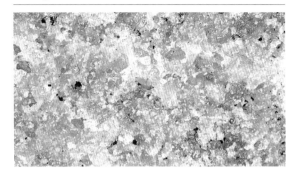

Siliceous sandstones often form hard and rather brittle rocks known as quartzites. They are sometimes called orthoquartzites to distinguish them from the quartzites formed by metamorphic processes. Such quartzites are formed by detrital grains of quartz, cemented together by crystalline quartz, often growing in crystalline continuity with the detrital grains. If pore spaces are still present, the detrital grains may display crystal faces and terminations, visible with a hand lens. More usually, they form an interlocking mosaic of quartz grains, which typically breaks across joints and other smooth fractures in the rock. Unless feldspar grains are present, the detrital grains are often difficult to distinguish.

Arkose × 2

Coarse-grained sandstones rich in feldspar are often known as arkoses. The detrital grains are usually angular in shape, and often vary in size, giving the rock a gritty texture, often enough to call it a grit. The feldspar is frequently microcline, orthoclase or perthite, imparting a pink or red colour to the rock, emphasized by the iron-rich nature of its cement. Arkoses resemble granites and granite-gneisses in mineral composition, from which they are often derived by physical disintegration with hardly any chemical weathering. Rapid erosion under an arid climate is suggested, followed by deposition as alluvial fans along the foot of rising mountains.

Greywacke

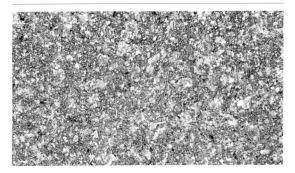

Greywacke is an impure sandstone consisting of quartz and feldspar grains, together with abundant rock fragments, set in a much finer-grained matrix of clay minerals, chlorite and carbonate. It is usually dark grey. The detrital grains are often rather angular, and poorly sorted, while the matrix is usually so altered that it now binds them together into a hard and very tough rock. If fine-grained, the detrital grains and rock fragments are often difficult to tell apart, giving a characteristic appearance to the rock, as shown here. Greywackes were most likely deposited from turbidity currents, and often in graded beds, displaying an extraordinary variety of sedimentary structures.

Pebbly Greywacke

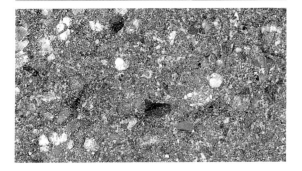

Once known as haggis rock in Scotland, pebbly greywackes are coarse-grained enough to show the presence of light-coloured quartz and feldspar grains, together with darker rock fragments, set in a matrix of much finer-grained material. Potash feldspar typically occurs as orthoclase and microcline, but sodic plagioclase may be present, along with such minerals as amphibole, pyroxene and garnet. The rock fragments include chert, jasper and a wide variety of volcanic and metamorphic rocks. All these features suggest that greywackes are derived from the rapid uplift and erosion of a terrain consisting of many different rock types. The eroded material is then deposited just as quickly in deep water by turbidity currents.

Siltstones

Siltstone is a sedimentary rock, finer-grained than a sandstone, but more coarse-grained than a shale, formed by detrital particles between 1/256mm and 1/16mm in size. Typically, siltstones are rather pale-coloured rocks, as shown here, interbedded with darker shales. The separate grains in the rock are often just visible under a hand lens, suggesting that the rock is granular in texture, but they are usually quite impossible to identify. They consist mostly of very small chips of quartz, feldspar and calcite, together with small flakes of white mica. This makes the rock resemble a very fine-grained sandstone with a siliceous appearance, rather than a shale or a mudstone with an earthy texture.

Flagstones

Siltstones are commonly very well-bedded rocks on a small scale. Such rocks were once quarried as flagstones if they could be split easily along the bedding into thin slabs. Very thin slabs were made into roofing slates, while slightly thicker varieties were used as paving stones. Apart from micaceous sandstones and flaggy quartzites, calcareous siltstones often make the best flagstones, like those once worked in Caithness from the lacustrine sediments of the Old Red Sandstone. As shown here, they are formed by very regular layers of pale-coloured siltstone, separated from one another by darker seams of more shaly material, together with brown-weathering beds of calcareous siltstone.

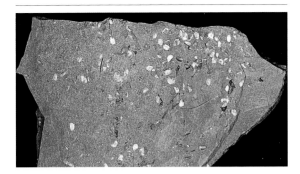

Shales and mudstones are extremely fine-grained sedimentary rocks, mostly consisting of clay particles less than $\frac{1}{256}$mm in diameter. Produced originally by chemical weathering, especially of feldspar, clay particles eventually settle out in still water as mud, often on the sea floor. Such a muddy sediment first forms a soft and sticky clay before all its water is driven out by ever-increasing loads of sedimentary rock, converting it into mudstone or shale. Shales are more fissile rocks than mudstones, splitting easily along the bedding into thin sheets, and forming paper shales if particularly fissile. Shown here is an ostracod shale, preserving the calcareous valves of a crustacean as fossils.

Black Shale $\times$ 1

Mudstone and shale vary greatly in colour, typically occurring in shades of grey, green, red, purple and black, according to circumstances. Black shales are unusually rich in carbonaceous matter. Most likely formed by organic processes, black shale is only preserved in reducing environments without any free oxygen, typical of deposition in sedimentary basins where the circulation of sea water is inhibited. Where organic matter is lacking, the mudstones and shales deposited under such conditions are often greenish-grey, rather than black, owing to the presence of ferrous iron. Nodules and concretions are a common feature in many dark-coloured mudstones and shales, formed by pyrite, calcite, dolomite and siderite.

Marl is a calcareous shale or mudstone, which is typically soft and rather friable. It is often grey in colour, and very finely grained with a blocky structure. However, the name has been used rather indiscriminately in the past for a variety of different rock types: the Keuper marl shown here with reduction spots contains less than 10% calcite. The rock becomes a marlstone if it is hard and compact, while it passes into an argillaceous (clay-rich) limestone if calcite makes up more than two-thirds of the rock. Such rocks are known as cementstones if they have a composition suitable for making cement. Often, they are dolomitic in composition.

Coals and Coal Seams

Coal is formed by the gradual accumulation of plant material under oxygen-free conditions, leading to waterlogged deposits of peat, rich in decaying wood and other vegetation. Once buried by the further deposition of sedimentary rock, this material is gradually converted into coal, losing water and other volatile constituents as it undergoes compaction. Brown coals and lignites are formed first, then bituminous coals, and finally anthracite, as temperature and pressure increase with depth. Brown coal is soft and dull with an earthy texture, and plant remains can easily be seen. Bituminous coal is hard and black with shiny layers, while anthracite is bright and lustrous with a conchoidal fracture.

Coal seams are rarely exposed today, since most have already been exploited for fuel over past centuries. Even so, their former presence may be inferred wherever seat-earths and fireclays are encountered, overlain by dark shales. They are typically rather pale-coloured and fine-grained rocks, and occur as fossil soils below coal seams, preserving the traces of plant roots. They owe their distinctive appearance to the leaching of alkalies, iron and magnesium by the growth of plants from the rock. Fireclay is a variety of seat-earth which can be used as a refractory material, able to withstand very high temperatures without melting.

Ganister

Ganister is a highly siliceous and very compact sandstone, often rather fine-grained, which has a typically leached appearance, giving it a pale colour. It is usually composed of angular grains of quartz, cemented together by secondary silica. It consists almost entirely of quartz, and once formed a fossil soil beneath a coal seam. All the other minerals in the original sediment have been destroyed as plants extracted the trace elements needed for their growth. It often shows the traces of their roots as coaly streaks in the rock. Its great purity allows it to be used as a refractory material, often for the hearths of blast furnaces. The name was originally applied to rocks of this type occurring around Sheffield.

Limestones

Limestones are carbonate-rich rocks composed chiefly of calcite, which has either been abstracted from sea water by organisms for making their shells and other hard parts, or precipitated rather more directly by the evaporation of sea water. Dolomites are mostly limestones in which the calcite was subsequently replaced by the mineral dolomite, but they are often difficult to distinguish from limestones in the field. Many limestones are rather coarse-grained rocks, sometimes displaying a crystalline texture, but other varieties are extremely fine grained, occurring as limestone muds. They often appear greyish in colour, particularly on fresh surfaces, but they can be white, cream, yellow, red, brown or even black.

Limestone Weathering

Limestone is a rock which dissolves rather easily in rain water, if the water carries carbon dioxide in solution to form a weak acid, capable of attacking calcite. This produces a distinctive landscape known as karst, with its flat-lying outcrops forming limestone pavements, broken by deep clefts. Acid rain water running down limestone often dissolves away the rock to make an intricately fretted surface with very sharp edges. Typically, limestone makes fertile ground, covered with grass, as it breaks down into soils capable of supporting a rich flora of lime-loving plants, unlike the acid soils developed on sandstone and quartzite, which often support only heather and bracken.

Organic limestones are formed by the remains of once-living organisms, such as foraminifera, corals, bryozoans, calcareous algae, crinoids, echinoids, brachiopods, bivalves and gastropods, whose shells or other hard parts now consist of calcite, even if they were once aragonite. Often, the rock is composed by one particular fossil, giving rise to shelly limestones, crinoidal limestones, nummulitic limestones and so on, set in a matrix of calcite. A loosely cemented shelly limestone is known in North America as a coquina (Spanish: *coquina*, a shell), while cornbrash is a coarse-grained shelly limestone of Jurassic age in England, which breaks down easily into brash, once used for liming cornfields.

Reef Limestone × 1

Reef limestones are formed by massive accumulations of calcareous fossils, such as corals, brachiopods, crinoids, bryozoans and calcareous algae, which are often found preserved in the position of their growth. Typically, limestone reefs have a solid framework, formed by the shells or skeletons of organisms like corals and rudist brachiopods, which were once attached to the sea floor, but which are now found encrusted and bound together by other calcite-secreting organisms. Any remaining spaces within this framework are commonly filled with extremely fine-grained lime-mud, or much coarser-grained sparry calcite. Often, the rock is now dolomite rather than limestone. It typically appears massive, lacking any sign of bedding.

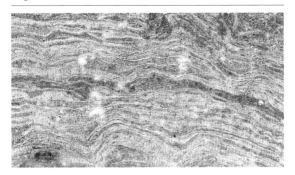

Algal limestones are typically finely bedded rocks, composed of thin layers of very fine-grained limestone up to a few millimetres in thickness. The layering is defined by slight differences in grain size of the sediment. It is most likely formed by mats of blue-green algae, trapping with their filaments each slight influx of coarser-grained sediment as deposition proceeds. Often, the layering appears slightly wavy or corrugated, thickening over any small irregularities in the underlying surface. The algal structures known as stromatolites can be recognized wherever these slight irregularities become much more pronounced, forming low mounds, rounded domes, and taller columns. They are often found in Precambrian limestones.

Chalk

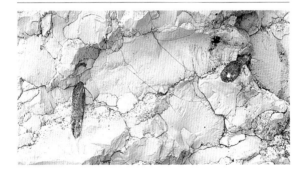

Chalk typically occurs as a very fine-grained and whitish limestone with a porous texture. It forms a thick and very widespread deposit of Cretaceous age, which can be traced from southeast England and northwest France into Scotland, Ireland, The Netherlands, Denmark, Germany and Sweden. Consisting almost entirely of calcite, it is composed of minute disc-like particles known as coccoliths, which once formed a protective sheath around algae, together with the remains of calcareous foraminifera and other free-swimming micro-organisms. Sponge spicules and radiolarian skeletons are also found in the chalk, consisting of silica rather than calcite. Shown here is a more indurated rock than usual, containing belemnite guards.

Oolitic limestone is formed by the direct precipitation of calcium carbonate from sea water, perhaps aided by the activity of calcareous algae. It consists of small, rounded particles, known as ooliths, up to 2mm in diameter, packed so closely together that they look like fish roe, hence their name (Greek: *oon*, an egg). Similar deposits occur today where calcium carbonate is being precipitated as aragonite in clear and shallow waters off the Bahamas, gradually building up concentric shells around quartz grains or shell fragments as they are washed to and fro by the waves. Larger grains are known as pisoliths (Greek: *pisos*, a pea), forming pisolitic limestone or pea-grit.

Nodular Limestone (Griotte)

Limestones quite often display a nodular structure in which irregular masses or nodules of even-grained limestone are separated by partings, often carrying a film of shaly material, or surrounded by shaly limestone of a different character. Nodular limestones apparently have a variety of different origins. Shown here is a very fine-grained nodular limestone of Devonian or Carboniferous age, which was deposited very slowly in deep water on a submarine plateau. Known as a griotte (French: a variety of cherry), it is cut by thin seams of reddish clay, which most likely accumulated during long pauses in the deposition of the limestone itself. Bedding dips to the right.

Dolomite

Dolomite is often difficult to distinguish from limestone except that calcite readily effervesces in dilute hydrochloric acid even when cold, while dolomite only does so feebly unless the acid is heated. Dolomite is not now secreted by any living organism, and it can only be precipitated from sea water under conditions of extreme salinity. Most dolomites were, therefore, probably formed from limestone after its deposition as magnesia-rich brines converted the original calcite into dolomite. If this occurred soon after deposition, the original features of the limestone are often preserved, but otherwise dolomite typically occurs as a massive and rather granular rock with sugary or saccharoidal texture, often weathering to a orangey-brown crust.

Silicified Limestone   × 1

The calcite in some limestones is occasionally replaced by quartz, giving rise to a silicified limestone if the process is complete. Often, silicification may only affect the calcareous fossils present in the rock. Such silicified fossils often weather proud of the surrounding limestone, which otherwise remains unaltered (*see* Corals, page 70). Oolites may also be preferentially affected by silicification, while chert and flint nodules in the chalk and other limestones are formed by much the same process. More rarely, the whole rock is affected, as shown by this example of a shelly limestone. It is most likely that silicification affects limestones soon after their deposition, before they are converted into solid rock.

Calcrete (or Cornstone)

Calcrete is a calcareous rock analogous to the caliche of semi-arid regions, which is a carbonate-rich soil formed where there is more evaporation than rainfall. Calcretes typically form as distinct layers of calcareous nodules, often several feet in thickness, lying along the bedding of fine-grained sandstones or siltstones. Red in colour, these sediments were most likely deposited on the flood plains of large rivers in semi-arid regions. The pale-coloured and often quite irregular nodules consist of fine-grained limestone, up to several centimetres in diameter. Calcretes were once known as cornstones, so called from the fertile soils which they produce, used for the growing of corn, particularly around Hereford in England.

Stalactites and Stalagmites

Stalactites and stalagmites are formed as spectacular features in limestone caverns wherever lime-rich water dripping from the roof loses carbon dioxide to the air, so allowing calcite to come out of solution to form calcareous tufa. Stalactites (Greek: *stalasso*, to drip) are the icicle-like masses descending from the roofs of limestone caverns, while stalagmites (Greek: *stalagma*, a dripping) are the more irregular masses formed on the floors of such caverns, deposited by water dripping from the roof. Stalactites and stalagmites eventually join up to form columns, ribbons and walls of calcium carbonate. Similar deposits of dripstone often occur where lime-rich water runs down the walls of limestone caverns.

Calcareous Tufa

Calcium carbonate is often deposited as calcareous tufa from waters in limestone terrains, which are rich in lime, and especially where the flow is turbulent, such as around springs and along river courses. It is a spongy and distinctly porous rock, perhaps secreted by calcareous algae, and often deposited on the leaves and stems of plants, which then rot away to leave their impressions in the rock. It typically forms whenever carbon dioxide comes out of solution, allowing calcium carbonate to be precipitated. If it is deposited along rivers it may gradually build up barriers over which waterfalls and rapids cascade into deep pools. These barriers occasionally dam back the waters of quite large lakes.

Travertine

Travertine is a hard, compact variety of calcareous tufa, typically deposited in volcanic regions around hot springs and geysers. It is usually light in colour, often white, but is sometimes coloured yellow, brown or even red by impurities such as iron, and it typically displays a delicately banded structure with a fibrous texture. It commonly occurs as rounded masses or irregular layers, often of considerable extent, building up wide terraces around hot springs. Similar rocks may also be formed by silica rather than calcium carbonate, occurring as deposits of siliceous sinter.

Any sedimentary rock containing more than 15% iron, allowing it to be worked as an iron ore, is known as an ironstone. Bog iron ores are soft and porous deposits, composed of rusty brown limonite, now forming in shallow lakes and bogs. Most other iron ores are sedimentary rocks, unusually rich in iron, making the rock distinctly heavy. Precambrian ironstones are finely banded with layers of haematite or magnetite alternating with quartz-rich cherts, now often recrystallized. More recent ironstones frequently occur as oolitic deposits and mudstones, composed of a variety of iron-bearing minerals, but often so badly weathered at the surface that their original nature is difficult to determine.

Black-band Ironstone

Siderite as iron carbonate ($FeCO_3$) sometimes occurs in sufficient quantity in mudstones and Carboniferous shales in west Europe and North America to form workable deposits, known as black-band ironstones, often associated with coal seams. The siderite typically occurs as extremely fine-grained nodules, as well as more continuous layers, lying along the bedding. The nodules have dark-grey interiors, weathering on the outside to a brownish crust. They are distinctly heavy for a sedimentary rock. If altered to a brownish colour, such sideritic mudstones and shales are known as clayband ironstones.

Any phosphate present in sedimentary rocks is usually the crypto-crystalline form of apatite known as collophane. As the main constituent of vertebrate bones, fish scales and shark's teeth, it is found widely scattered through sedimentary rocks, occasionally accumulating as fossil bone-beds where currents have swept away all the other sediment. Otherwise, most phosphate occurs as nodules, as illustrated, often well-rounded by currents, in which fossils are commonly embedded. They may be encrusted with oysters and other fossils. They are typically dark grey or black in Mesozoic rocks, often displaying a bloom of paler blue, but orange or brown in younger rocks, with a greenish coating.

Cherts

Chert is a compact, very hard and extremely fine-grained rock, which cannot be easily scratched with a knife. It consists of crypto-crystalline silica, typically occurring as chalcedony, coloured red, green or black by impurities, but sometimes whitish with a blue opalescent tinge. Although some cherts are finely bedded rocks, others occur as nodular masses and concretions, particularly in limestones and some shales. The silica in bedded cherts may be derived from micro-organisms such as radiolaria and diatoms, together with some sponges, which are able to secrete silica to form their hard parts. Such microfossils can be seen through a hand lens as minute specks up to 0.25mm across in radiolarian cherts.

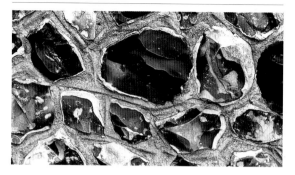

Flint is a dark variety of chert, which weathers to a pale crust, typically found as nodules in chalk. It usually has a conchoidal fracture, which made it suitable for use as Neolithic arrow-heads, while chert tends to splinter, forming flat fractures. The chert and flint nodules that occur in limestones and some other rocks are secondary in origin, replacing the original material of the rock. They may nucleate on fossils, such as sponges and echinoids, which then become embedded at their centres, or they may replace more porous rock, such as animal burrows. The silica in these nodules is most likely derived from the solution of sponge spicules and other siliceous microfossils in the original rock.

Jasper

Jasper is a dense variety of cryptocrystalline silica SiO_2, usually bright red in colour but sometimes yellow, brown, green or black, which owes its colouring to the presence of finely disseminated iron compounds in the rock. It is often regarded as a variety of chalcedony, but many examples may just be extremely fine-grained quartz. Jasper is commonly found associated with pillow lavas, filling in the spaces between the individual pillows, as shown here. Silica and iron oxides were presumably derived from emanations given off by the lava as it cooled down. Some varieties, known as Egyptian or ribbon jasper, are beautifully banded with different shades of brown (*see also* page 22).

Evaporites (Gypsum)

Evaporites are sedimentary rocks composed of gypsum, anhydrite and rock-salt (halite), together with other less common minerals. They are typically formed as chemical precipitates by the evaporation of sea water in enclosed basins, separated from the open sea by a low-lying bar or threshold. Owing to their solubility, such rocks are rarely seen at the surface, except in arid climates, or where denudation has been especially rapid. Even then, gypsum is only likely to be encountered, usually as nodular masses of fine-grained crystals, together with thin veins of satin spar, interbedded with red shales and marls. By dissolving away, thicker beds of evaporites often produce collapse breccias, affecting the overlying strata.

Satin Spar and Nodular Gypsum

Above: *Satin Spar*
Below: *Nodular Gypsum (field of view 30cm)*

Satin spar typically occurs as thin veins of fibrous gypsum with a silky sheen. It is found as a vein filling, deposited from watery solutions percolating through a fracture as its walls were pushed apart by hydrostatic pressure. Such veins are often associated with nodular masses of fine-grained gypsum, which often occur as discrete layers in the rock. The nodules may be so closely packed together that they are only separated by thin stringers of fine-grained sediment, making the rock appear like chicken wire. If extremely fine-grained, gypsum deposits may be worked as alabaster, which is an ornamental stone, ivory-white in colour but often stained with hydrated iron oxides. It is capable of taking a fine polish.

FOSSILS

Fossils are the remains of ancient plants and animals preserved in sedimentary rocks. The soft tissues of animals are rarely preserved as they decay very rapidly after death, even if not eaten by scavengers. If they are preserved, only impressions are left. It is therefore the hard parts of shelly or bony animals which are more commonly preserved as **body fossils**, together with the woody impressions made by plant tissues. The tracks, trails and burrows made by individual animals, and their excreta, may also be preserved, forming what are known as **trace fossils**.

Fossils are only likely to be preserved by rapid burial. This occurs typically on the sea floor, or less commonly in rivers and lakes, rather than on the land where weathering and erosion are the dominant processes. Terrestrial plants and animals are therefore less commonly found as fossils, compared with marine organisms, especially invertebrate shelled animals.

Fossilization Once buried by sediment, the remains of plants and animals are often altered in some way. Woody plants are usually converted into thin films of carbonaceous matter, as the volatile components of cellulose, such as water, oxygen, hydrogen and nitrogen, are driven off by heat and pressure. Often better preserved is horny chitin or its equivalent, which variously forms the hard parts of insects, inarticulate brachiopods, trilobites and graptolites.

Where shells were originally formed by aragonite, this usually reverts to calcite as the more stable form of calcium carbonate, while calcite itself may recrystallize. Percolating solutions often deposit mineral matter within fossil bones and shells if they are porous, or replace the original shell with entirely different minerals, such as silica or pyrite.

Stratigraphic dating Giving us the only direct evidence of evolutionary change, fossils allow the dating of sedimentary rocks according to the **stratigraphic time-scale** (*see* table, page 5). The sudden appearance of hard-bodied animals at the start of Cambrian times around 570 million years ago distinguishes the Phanerozoic era from the Precambrian. Organic life then started to evolve rapidly so that nearly all the invertebrate groups now present in the fossil record appeared within the next 100 million years.

The rapid evolution of so many fossil species, coupled with their eventual extinction, resulted in the unique fossil assemblages so characteristic of the various geological periods in the Phanerozoic era. These periods divide up the stratigraphic or geological column into separate systems, occurring one after another during the course of geological history, thus giving the stratigraphic age of the rocks.

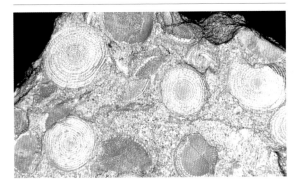

These simple animals with only a single cell are mostly preserved as microfossils less than 1mm across. Occasionally, larger forms occur, such as the calcareous foraminifera known as *Nummulites*, as shown here. Its disc-like shell may be split apart to reveal a series of sequential chambers, each once occupied by the organism, and now found coiled into a spiral. Nummulitic limestones of Tertiary age are common around the Mediterranean, and occur in Egypt, where such rocks were used in building the Pyramids. The only other group of geological importance within the Protozoa are the radiolaria with siliceous shells, which occur in the radiolarian cherts.

Sponges × 1

The simplest of multi-cellular animals, known as the Porifera (Cambrian to Recent), sponges are only preserved as fossils if they have a horny or chitinous skeleton, which may be strengthened by calcareous or siliceous spicules. As shown here, they are often shaped like a vase, supported by a narrow stalk which anchored the animal to its substratum. Fossil sponges also make bulbous masses, encrusting other fossils. Perhaps related to the sponges are the Stromatoporoids (Cambrian to Cretaceous), which make up rounded masses of calcareous matter in limestone reefs.

Bryozoa (Ordovician to Recent) are aquatic organisms living in small colonies of many tiny individuals. Each animal lives in a tube-like chamber with perforated walls, which it constructs out of chitin or calcareous material. These chambers are arranged in many different ways, often building up sheet-like encrustations on rocks, shells and even seaweed, which often look like corals, or branching out into frond-like or bushy masses, which are sometimes fan-shaped or stick-like. Their surface typically has a lacy appearance, as illustrated. They are usually only preserved as fossils if they have calcareous skeletons, when they often occur as important reef-builders.

Worms   × 1.5

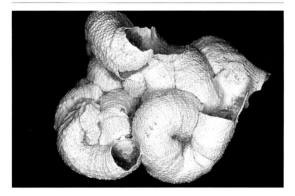

Worms are typically soft-bodied animals without any hard parts, except that some species have horny jaws. However, they may live in burrows lined with sand grains and shell fragments. Other species secrete calcareous tubes which they inhabit, often forming irregular masses which may be attached to rocks, shells and other objects on the sea floor, forming worm tubes. However, what are often called worm tubes are the burrows of a wide variety of different animals, even if they are difficult or impossible to identify with any certainty. The example above displays a delicate ornament on its surface.

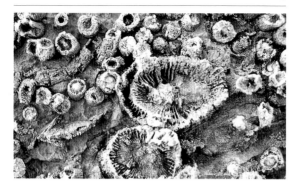

Corals (Ordovician to Recent) are preserved as calcareous skeletons, originally secreted by a simple animal known as a polyp. Its sack-like body had an internal cavity which acted as its stomach. There was only a single opening to the outside, surrounded by tentacles. The polyp sat in a cup-like depression on top of its calcareous skeleton, or corallite, which it built upwards to form a support as it grew. Corals are classified according to their internal structure, which cannot often be observed directly. Shown here in cross-section are two distinct species of corals, now silicified, which have weathered proud of the surrounding limestone.

Solitary Corals × 1.5

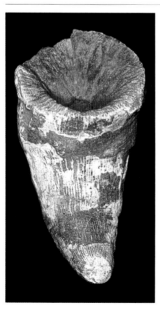

Solitary corals consist of a single corallite, which typically grew to a large size. They display a cylindrical tube shape in some species, but more commonly appear horn-like, conical in shape, but often slightly curved as shown here. The exterior surface of the corallite may be wrinkled with horizontal corrugations, especially in the Rugose corals (Ordovician to Permian). Typically, internal partitions known as septa divide the corallite radially along its length, often leaving their traces on its exterior surface and fusing along its axis to form a central column. The manner in which the septa are inserted is a feature that helps to distinguish Rugose corals from Scleractinian corals (Triassic to Recent).

Colonial corals grew by the repeated budding of a single polyp to form a complex skeleton composed of many separate corallites, so forming a colony. If closely packed together, the corallites typically have straight walls in contact with one another, giving a polygonal pattern in cross-section. However, these walls may be lost in some species, leaving only a central column with radiating septa as their internal structure. Corallites packed more loosely together typically have more rounded or elongate cross-sections, but form a tree-like colony with many different branches. Rugose and Scleractinian corals both occur as colonial forms.

Tabulate Corals   × 1.5

Tabulate corals (Ordovician to Carboniferous) are an extinct group of colonial corals, which get their name from the transverse plates of calcareous material, known as tabulae, which divide each corallite into a series of horizontal compartments along its length. The corallites were rarely more than several millimetres across, even if the colonies were very much larger. The corallites lack the internal structures found in other corals, apart from rudimentary septa in some species. However, tabulae are a common feature in Rugose corals, even if they are lacking in the Scleractinian corals. Shown here is *Halysites*, commonly known as the chain coral.

Brachiopods (Cambrian to Recent) are marine organisms with two shells, hinged together to enclose the animal. While each shell is bilaterally symmetrical, they typically differ in size and shape from one another, as is shown here. Most species lived attached to the sea floor by a fleshy stalk, which passed out through an aperture in the larger valve, close to the beak, or through an opening between the paired valves. Other species lived partly buried in mud, sometimes in burrows, but usually anchored to the sea floor by spines on the back of the larger valve, or cemented by this valve to the underlying substratum.

Articulate Brachiopods × 1.5

Taxonomically, brachiopods are divided into two classes (articulate and inarticulate) according to how their shells were hinged together. Articulate brachiopods have calcareous shells that are joined together by two teeth lying along the hinge line of the larger shell, which fit into sockets in a corresponding position on the smaller shell. The two shells are opened and closed by two sets of muscles, so allowing the animal to feed. The shells vary in shape from rounded to more elongate forms, often with narrow 'wings', as the hinge line increases in length. Although some species have smooth shells, many species display a radial ribbing as well as concentric growth lines, as can be seen here.

Inarticulate brachiopods differ from the articulate species described on the previous page in lacking a well-designed hinge line equipped with teeth and sockets. Instead, reaching their acme by the end of the Cambrian, they existed as more primitive forms in which the two shells were simply held together by several pairs of muscles. Their shells are usually composed of chitin rather than calcite, often appearing like mother-of-pearl, and lacking much ornamentation, apart from sets of fine lines. Shown here is the burrowing form known as *Lingula* (Ordovician to Recent). It had a long stalk which could be contracted, allowing it to withdraw into its burrow, which it occupied in muddy sediment.

Bivalves × 0.5

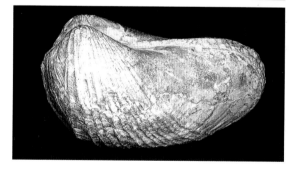

Bivalves (Cambrian to Recent) are a group of molluscs which includes such everyday shellfish as cockles, scallops, razor-shells, mussels, oysters and clams. They resemble brachiopods in possessing two shells, usually made of aragonite rather than calcite, hinged to enclose the living animal. They differ from brachiopods since these two shells are usually the same size and shape, typically occurring as mirror images of one another, except in the mussels and oysters, which lived cemented to the sea floor. Each shell tends to be asymmetrical, apart from such free-swimming exceptions as *Pecten*. The bivalves are adapted to various modes of life, so there is no simple scheme for their classification.

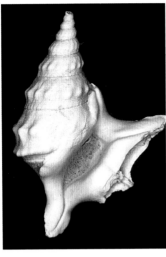

Gastropods (Cambrian to Recent) are another well-known group of molluscs, which includes animals such as slugs, snails, winkles, whelks, cowries and limpets. They typically make a shell of aragonite with only a single chamber, which is coiled upwards into a twisted spiral. Gastropods vary greatly in the shape and ornamentation they exhibit. This makes the extinct forms very difficult to classify, since species belonging to different groups often resemble each other. Their appearance can vary from turreted forms with slender whorls to squatter forms with fatter whorls. Other species are coiled into flat spirals, often with overlapping whorls, which are easily confused with the shape typical of ammonites.

Belemnites   × 1

Belemnites (Triassic to early Tertiary) are the fossils left by an extinct group of molluscs, which are now preserved as massive objects with very smooth surfaces, shaped like a cigar or a bullet, and known as guards. The animal resembled a squid or cuttlefish, and its guard was enclosed within its body. The guard is composed of fibrous crystals of calcite, arranged radially at right angles to its length. Its weight probably served to keep the animal horizontal as it moved through the water. Rarely preserved is the shelly phragmacone, which fitted into a conical indentation at the blunt end of the guard.

Nautiloids

Another nearly extinct group of molluscs are the Nautiloids (Cambrian to Recent), today only represented by *Nautilus*, which lives in the surface waters of the southwest Pacific. Although its shell is coiled into a flat spiral, earlier nautiloids mostly had straight shells, as shown here by *Orthoceras* (Ordovician to Triassic). The shell is divided internally into chambers by partitions, known as septa. Saucer-like, they make a smooth or slightly sinuous trace against the inner wall of the shell, known as the suture. A central aperture in each septa allowed an organ to release gas into the chambers no longer inhabited by the animal, so making it buoyant.

Goniatites

× 0.33

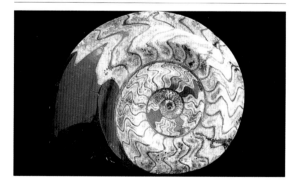

Goniatites (Devonian to Permian) were the precursors of the Ammonites, which flourished in the Jurassic and Cretaceous. Both represent now-extinct groups of molluscs, which have a calcareous shell partitioned by septa into internal chambers like those of their ancestors, the Nautiloids. They typically have a coiled shell, although some groups, such as Gastropods, make helicoidal shells while others have straight shells, sometimes with a coiled first segment. Goniatites have simple zig-zag sutures, formed by the septa meeting the inner wall of the outer shell. These can be seen if the outer shell is removed, leaving a cast of its interior.

Ammonites (Jurassic to Cretaceous) only differ from the earlier Goniatites (and other related groups) in the greater complexity shown by their suture-lines. Highly irregular in form, they are thrown into elaborate frills and plications along their length. Ammonites often have rather plump shells with the outer whorls tending to overlap the inner ones, so forming a hollow umbilicus at their centre. Other species show hardly any overlap, so forming a rather flatter shell in which all the whorls are clearly visible. The shell is often heavily ornamented by radial ribs, while a sharp-edged keel may run around its outer edge.

Echinoids (Sea-urchins)   × 2

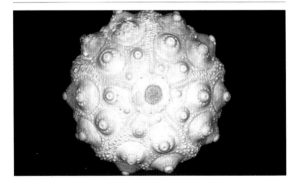

Echinoids (Ordovician to Recent) have spiny skeletons, known as a test, consisting of a polygonal mosaic of interlocking plates, each formed by a single crystal of calcite. Typically, the test makes a rounded body with a flattened base. It consists of five rows of small plates, each pierced by pores, arranged in pairs, and separated from one another by five rows of larger plates, also arranged in pairs. They encircle the test, radiating from a small cluster of plates on its upper surface, which surrounds the anus of the animal, and meeting again around a larger opening underneath the animal, which is its mouth.

Irregular Echinoids (Heart-urchins)

Irregular echinoids (Jurassic to Recent) are mostly burrowing forms which adapted to this way of life by losing the radial symmetry typical of the regular echinoids. This occurs wherever the mouth and anus are no longer placed centrally. The anus in particular migrates backwards away from the point where the rows of plates still meet one another on the upper surface of the test. It often lies in a sunken groove. The mouth may move forward to a rather similar position at the front. It usually but not always lies where the five alternating sets of plates meet one another opposite the anus.

Crinoids (Sea-lilies) × 0.75

Crinoids (Ordovician to Recent) typically lived attached by a long stalk to the sea bed, except for some recent forms, which are free-swimming. They are rarely preserved as complete fossils, since their skeletons readily disintegrated after death, giving rise to crinoidal limestones. The stem was made up of crinoid ossicles, typically shaped like squat round discs, each formed by a single crystal of calcite. The stem ended in the calyx, made up of a few large plates, where the animal lived. The calyx had a fringe of five arms, made up of more ossicles, which often branched repeatedly upwards, making crinoids look like plants, hence their popular name of sea-lilies.

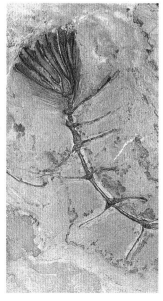

Graptolites

× 1.5

Graptolites (Cambrian to Carboniferous) are a puzzling group of marine organisms, possibly ancestral to the vertebrates. They formed colonies of separate individuals or polyps, each living in a small conical cup, made of chitin, arranged singly or grouped in pairs to form a thin fragile skeleton. Dendroid graptolites occurred as complex colonies with up to sixty-four branches, but the more advanced groups had first eight, then four or two branches, and eventually only a single branch. They typically occur as carbonaceous streaks in the rock, marked by a series of notches, and look like pencil marks, hence their name (Greek: *graptos*, marked with letters).

Trilobites

× 2

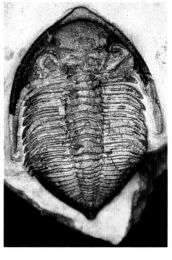

Trilobites (Cambrian to Permian) are fossil arthropods, a group which includes the more familiar insects and crustaceans. They had segmented skeletons, which consisted possibly of chitin strengthened by calcite forming an outer carapace. Trilobites had a distinct head-shield, which often carried a pair of compound eyes, although some species were blind; a segmented thorax capable of articulation; and a shield-like tail-region. There was a raised axis along the centre of the body, flanked by two furrows, from which the animal's name is derived. The tail often resembled the thorax except that its segments were fused together. However, it may be smooth, in which case it looks more like the head-shield.

Vertebrates (Ordovician to Recent) are rarely preserved as fossils. Usually single bones are found rather than complete skeletons, which tend to break up after death. In fact, the vertebrate remains most likely to be encountered are fish scales and shark teeth, although well-preserved skeletons of fossil fish may occur in great abundance at a particular horizon, known as a fish-bed. Reptiles and amphibians are equally rare, especially the species that lived mostly on land. The same is true of birds, since they have an easily destroyed skeleton with very light bones. Fossil mammals are rarely found, since they only occur in any abundance in Pleistocene deposits, and then only locally.

Fish Scales and Shark Teeth

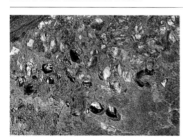

Fish Scales × 1

Below:
Shark Tooth × 0.75

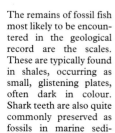

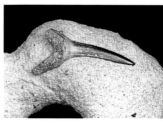

The remains of fossil fish most likely to be encountered in the geological record are the scales. These are typically found in shales, occurring as small, glistening plates, often dark in colour. Shark teeth are also quite commonly preserved as fossils in marine sediments, particularly as sharks repeatedly shed their teeth during life. The teeth display a characteristic form, tapering to a sharp point from a triangular base, often with serrated edges.

IGNEOUS ROCKS

Igneous rocks have their origin deep within the Earth, where the temperatures are high enough for rocks to melt. If this molten material, known as **magma**, penetrates upwards to reach the Earth's surface, it erupts as **lava** from volcanoes, cooling down and then solidifying to form **lava flows**. Alternatively, magma in its upward ascent may cool down and solidify at depth to form **igneous intrusions**, surrounded by their pre-existing **country-rocks**. They are only exposed at the Earth's surface if erosion subsequently strips off the overlying rocks.

Some igneous intrusions occupy vertical fractures which the magma forced apart as it flowed upwards, forming a wall-like mass known as a **dyke**. Other intrusions are formed where magma, flowing horizontally along the bedding of sedimentary rocks, lifts up the overlying rocks to form a sheet-like mass known as a **sill**. Other minor intrusions are neither dykes nor sills, but occur as inclined **sheets** with parallel walls, or as vertical **plugs**, shaped like a cylinder. Very large masses of igneous rock, known as **stocks** and **batholiths**, often lack any obvious foundation of older rocks at depth, forming **plutons**. Such large intrusions frequently alter and metamorphose their country-rocks, forming **metamorphic aureoles** around their outcrops.

Columnar jointing in basaltic lava flow, Giant's Causeway, Antrim.

Grain size of igneous rocks If molten lava cools down so quickly that crystals have no time to form, it becomes quenched to form a **volcanic glass**. Such glasses often undergo devitrification, crystallizing out afterwards to form a very fine-grained rock. More usually, minerals start to crystallize out as the molten lava itself loses heat, so eventually forming a very fine-grained **volcanic rock** with a crystalline texture. Unless larger crystals were carried up from depth, giving rise to a **porphyritic** texture, the individual grains are hardly ever visible, even with a hand lens, since they are rarely more than 0.5mm in size.

Dykes, sills and other sheet-like intrusions resemble lava flows in that they usually cool down rapidly to form the relatively fine-grained **hyperbyssal rocks**, typically varying between 0.5mm and 1mm in grain size. Such intrusions often exhibit **chilled margins** against their country-rocks, marked by narrow selvedges of finer-grained or even glassy rock along their contacts. If the dyke itself is basalt, such a dark-coloured basaltic glass is known as **tachylyte**.

Batholiths and other deep-seated intrusions invariably cool down much more slowly, perhaps taking several million years to reach the temperature of their surroundings. By allowing only a small number of largish crystals to grow as the magma solidifies, rather than a multitude of much smaller ones, this typically produces a coarse-grained rock with the grains exceeding 5mm in size. The crystals in such a **plutonic rock** can easily be seen with the naked eye, even though they are best identified using a hand lens.

Naming igneous rocks Nearly all igneous rocks are composed of silicate minerals, in which silica (SiO_2) was originally thought to act as an acid, occurring in combination with other metallic oxides as its bases. Accordingly, igneous rocks were divided into acid and basic varieties. **Acid rocks** like granite and granodiorite are rich in silica, along with the alkalis of potash and soda, but poor in iron oxides, magnesia and lime. This typically gives a light-coloured rock rich in quartz and alkali feldspars, but lacking minerals such as pyroxene and olivine. **Basic rocks** like basalt are rich in iron oxides, magnesia and lime, but poor in silica and alkalis. This typically gives a dark-coloured rock without any free quartz, but rich in calcic feldspar and pyroxene. **Intermediate rocks** have a composition lying between acid and basic rocks, while **ultrabasic rocks** are deficient in silica, lacking any free quartz or even feldspar.

The further classification of igneous rocks depends on identifying the composition of their feldspars, which can only be done with any accuracy under the microscope. What name is given to the rock also depends on its grain size, whether there is any quartz or feldspathoid present in the rock, and what proportion of **ferromagnesian minerals,** rich in iron and magnesium, such as pyroxene or olivine in particular, along with biotite and hornblende, are also present.

Identification of igneous minerals Seen in the field, feldspar typically occurs in coarse-grained rocks as pale pink, whitish or greyish crystals with a porcellaneous appearance, often rather massive but showing a good cleavage. It can usually be distinguished quite easily from quartz, which has a 'glassy' appearance and lacks any cleavage. Quartz is slightly harder than feldspar, so that a knife can often scratch feldspar but not quartz.

Apart from biotite with its distinctive cleavage, ferromagnesian minerals are often difficult to distinguish from one another, although olivine if unaltered may display a distinctive colour. Amphiboles typically occur as elongate six-sided crystals with cleavages at 120°, while pyroxenes make more stubby eight-sided crystals with cleavages at 90°, but such features are often difficult to observe even with a hand lens.

Granite is a coarse-grained igneous rock of acid composition and consists essentially of quartz (often in amounts much greater than 10%) and alkali-feldspar, typically occurring as orthoclase, microcline and perthite, but also including albite. Apart from albite, found only in alkali-granite, any plagioclase feldspar present is usually oligoclase, rarely andesine. Minor amounts of biotite and hornblende are common, together with muscovite in some granites and occasionally pyroxenes, which give their name to the rock. Granites usually occur in pale shades of white, pink, red or grey as ferromagnesian minerals rarely make up more than 20% of the rock.

Granodiorite

×4

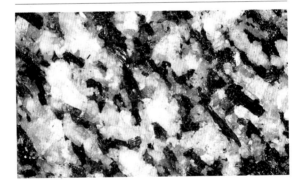

Granodiorite is a coarse-grained igneous rock, containing quartz as an essential mineral, which differs from granite in that sodic plagioclase is more abundant than potash feldspar, rather than vice versa. Greyish in colour, it often contains rather more ferromagnesian minerals than granite. Separating granite from granodiorite is Adamellite, in which sodic plagioclase and alkali feldspar are both present in roughly equal amounts. Shown here is a granodiorite with hornblende as its ferromagnesian mineral, rather than biotite, although both minerals often occur together. Granodiorites are even more abundant than granites, being the commonest of all plutonic rocks.

Muscovite- and Biotite-granite

Muscovite-granite is distinguished by the presence of muscovite, rather than biotite or hornblende. The top picture shows three crystals of silvery muscovite, each displaying a single direction of perfect cleavage. They are lying in a matrix of quartz and alkali feldspar together with some smaller flakes of biotite. Biotite-granite perhaps occurs even more commonly than muscovite-granite. It is distinguished by the presence of biotite, rather than muscovite or hornblende, which occasionally forms lar-

Above: *Muscovite-granite* × 0.5
Below: *Biotite-granite* × 4

gish crystals as shown in the centre of the photograph. It often occurs with muscovite, giving rise to muscovite-biotite granite, or hornblende, giving rise to hornblende-biotite-granite.

Hornblende-granite

× 4.4

Hornblende-granite can only be distinguished from other granites if hornblende can be recognized in the rock. Typically, its presence is revealed by the occurrence of dark-coloured grains, forming six-sided prisms with their prism faces at 120° to one another, as seen in cross-section (*see also* Granodiorite opposite). Hornblende often occurs with biotite, forming the very common rock type known as hornblende-biotite-granite, which otherwise typically displays the mineralogy of any other granite. Biotite occurs as a dark-coloured mineral with only a single cleavage, reflecting the light, which is often so perfect that cleavage flakes can be detached using a pin.

Granite sometimes has large crystals or phenocrysts of potash feldspar, set in a finer-grained matrix of alkali-feldspar and quartz, forming what is known as a porphyritic texture. The matrix of the rock is still sufficiently coarse-grained for it to be classed as a granite. Often, the feldspar phenocrysts are orthoclase, which may be identified by the presence of simple twins, dividing the crystals into two halves along their lengths, so that their cleavages lie at an angle to one another, reflecting the light differently. Unlike other porphyritic rocks in which the phenocrysts were carried up from the depths, these feldspar crystals most likely crystallized out as the rock solidified.

Rapakivi Granite × 2

Rapakivi texture occurs in alkali-granites and other acid igneous rocks wherever porphyritic crystals of potash feldspar are mantled by narrow rims of sodic plagioclase, often giving a whitish rim around a pinkish interior, sometimes in an alternating fashion. The rock itself is often known as a Rapakivi granite, since in Finland it forms a rock that easily disintegrates (Finnish: *rapakivi*, crumbly rock). The feldspar phenocrysts are often somewhat rounded, which perhaps suggests that they were partially absorbed by the magma before the rim of sodic plagioclase crystallized around them.

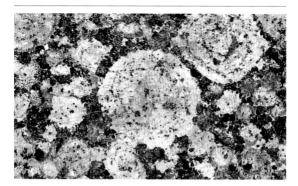

Orbicular texture is occasionally seen both in granites and more basic igneous rocks such as granodiorites and quartz-diorites. It consists of large ovoid bodies, often several centimetres in diameter, which are concentrically banded around a central nucleus, itself sometimes formed by a xenolith. Typically, these concentric layers consist of quartz and feldspar, alternating with layers richer in hornblende and biotite. Crystallization apparently started around this nucleus, and then built up the concentric structure by the rhythmic accretion of these layers, differing in mineral composition from one another. Polished slabs are often seen in shop fronts.

Drusy Granite × 0.75

Drusy granite contains small cavities of irregular shape, known as druses, formed by vapour separating out from the magma during the final stages of crystallization. The druses are usually lined by crystals of the surrounding rock, such as quartz and alkali feldspar, often projecting inwards with perfectly formed terminations, and much larger than elsewhere in the rock. Such rocks are typically found as high-level intrusions, which consolidated close to the Earth's surface under relatively low pressures. Some drusy granites are the source for well-formed crystals of semi-precious quartz, especially the variety of smoky quartz known as Cairngorm.

Xenolithic Granite

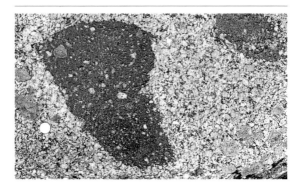

Xenolithic rocks are formed by igneous intrusions wherever they incorporate angular fragments of pre-existing rocks, forming xenoliths. Such fragments are typically derived from the country-rocks invaded by the igneous intrusion itself. They commonly occur in granitic rocks as patches of much darker rock. They frequently undergo thermal metamorphism, losing their angular outlines as they are gradually assimilated, first becoming rounded and then being absorbed into the magma. Shown here are dark-coloured xenoliths in which 'phenocrysts' of pink feldspar have grown, similar to the feldspar crystals occurring in the granite itself.

Greisen

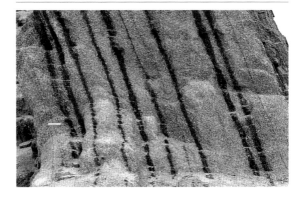

Granites are often altered chemically by volatile-rich gases at a high temperature, allowing new minerals to form as the result of pneumatolysis (Greek: *pneumatos*, air or gas). Greisen is typically formed by the alteration of granite by superheated steam rich in fluorine. It is a light-coloured rock of quartz and white mica, usually a lithium-bearing variety. Greisens are often associated with tinstone veins, carrying cassiterite together with topaz, white mica and quartz. Shown here are narrow veins of quartz-rich greisen formed by the alteration of granite along close-spaced fractures in the rock.

Tourmaline-bearing Granite

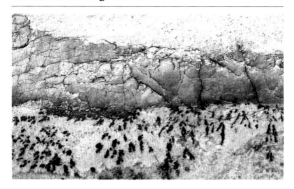

Pneumatolysis can also result in tourmaline-bearing rocks, formed by the alteration of granite resulting from the action of superheated steam carrying boron and fluorine. Tourmaline first takes the place of muscovite, while further alteration results in the replacement of feldspar by tourmaline and quartz. The example above shows a much-altered granite adjacent to a quartz vein, in which pneumatolysis has caused finger-like crystals of tourmaline to grow in the solid rock, producing a highly complex pattern. Tourmalinization may also affect the metamorphosed country-rocks surrounding a granite pluton.

Schorl-rock   ×2

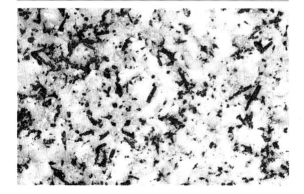

Schorl-rock is formed by the complete tourmalinization of all the micas and feldspars in a granite, leaving a rather granular rock consisting of quartz grains and prismatic crystals of tourmaline, without any feldspar (Cornish: *schorl*, tourmaline). Less intense alteration results in a rock known as luxullianite (not illustrated), in which porphyritic crystals of reddish feldspar are surrounded by a dark-blue groundmass of quartz, within which radiating sheaves of tourmaline needles are embedded. It was used for the tomb of the Duke of Wellington in St Paul's Cathedral, London.

Granite-pegmatite

Very coarse-grained rocks of igneous affinities are known as pegmatites if the crystals are more than 2.5cm in length. Granite-pegmatites typically consist of quartz and alkali feldspar in roughly equal amounts, along with well-formed crystals of muscovite and many other minerals, such as beryl, apatite, zircon, tourmaline, topaz and cassiterite, concentrated by the crystallization of a volatile-rich residuum, rich in trace elements. Giant crystals up to several metres in length are occasionally found. Granite-pegmatites typically occur as veins and more irregular masses, associated with granite intrusions, or cutting across their country-rocks. Shown here is a pegmatite with milky quartz and pink feldspar.

Graphic Granite ×2

Graphic texture is seen in granites wherever quartz occurs as a regular intergrowth with potash feldspar, forming wedge-shaped patches, which are said to resemble cuneiform or runic writing. It is thought to form by the simultaneous crystallization of both these minerals, or perhaps by the quartz replacing the potash feldspar selectively along certain planes. The rock formed by such an intergrowth is itself known as a graphic granite, although the texture is best seen in pegmatites. The medium-grained rock of granitic composition known as a granophyre displays much the same texture but only on a microscopic scale, rarely visible even using a hand lens.

Microgranite

Microgranite is an igneous rock of granitic composition, from which it is usually distinguished if its grains are less than 5mm in size. Unfortunately, there is little agreement among different authorities on what constitutes such a medium-grained igneous rock. Typically, rocks such as microgranite have a grain size less than that expected for a granite, while being too coarse-grained to be classified as a rhyolite or its intrusive equivalent. They are all named by taking their coarse-grained equivalent, and adding micro- as a prefix to its name. Such rocks may be distinguished from hyperbyssal rocks, which resemble their volcanic equivalents in grain size, but which are intrusive in nature.

Quartz-porphyry and Felsite

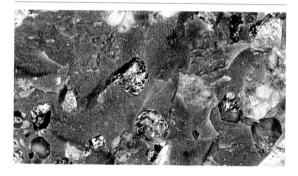

Quartz-porphyry is an intrusive rock of granitic composition in which conspicuous phenocrysts of quartz and alkali-feldspar are set in a much finer-grained matrix of the same minerals. Such rocks pass into felsites as the phenocrysts gradually become less abundant, typically forming a rather fine-grained rock with few distinctive features. Other intrusive rocks of granitic composition include microgranites and granophyres, in which the crystalline textures are visible to the naked eye even although the individual crystals often do not exceed 1–2mm in size, unless they occur as phenocrysts. All these rocks are typically light-coloured, especially on weathered surfaces, appearing greyish or sometimes a striking pink or red.

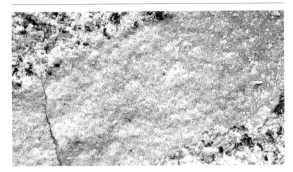

Aplites are very fine-grained, light-coloured rocks with an even-grained, saccharoidal or sugary texture, composed almost entirely of quartz and alkali-feldspar. They may also contain small amounts of tourmaline, topaz and fluorite, but rarely any biotite. Although they often occur on a small scale as separate intrusions in the form of narrow dykes, veins and sheets, closely associated with granite intrusions, they are sometimes found together with pegmatite, making up the same body. The pegmatite may occur as irregular patches of coarser-grained rock in the aplite, or it may occur as distinct layers, sometimes forming a fringe along the upper contact of the aplite. Shown here is an aplite cutting across granitic rock.

Flow-banded Rhyolite   × 2

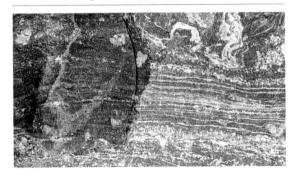

Rhyolite is the volcanic equivalent of granite, forming a very fine-grained rock of acid composition, which typically occurs as lava flows, often of considerable thickness. It consists essentially of quartz and alkali-feldspar, together with sodic plagioclase, which may all occur as phenocrysts set in a very fine-grained or even glassy matrix. Biotite may be present, occurring sparsely as corroded phenocrysts. Unless quartz can be recognized, it is often difficult to identify a particular rock as a rhyolite. Most rhyolites weather to a pale crust even if they appear dark on a fresh surface. They often exhibit flow-banding, as shown here, reflecting their highly viscous nature when molten.

Auto-brecciated Rhyolite

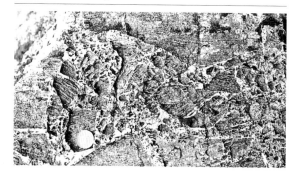

Autobrecciation is seen in rhyolites (and andesites) wherever the lava flow has broken up into angular fragments, cemented together by equally fine-grained material of much the same composition. Often, flow-banding is present within these fragments, suggesting that the process occurs as the lava becomes ever more viscous in cooling down, before it finally solidifies. Autobrecciation in andesites often appears to affect only the upper parts of the lava flows, suggesting that their already solid crusts break up even as they are carried along by the still-fluid lava of their interiors. The explosive escape of steam may explain the same phenomenon in rhyolites, perhaps triggered by the flow of rhyolite lava over water-saturated sediment.

Obsidian and Pitchstone   × 2

Obsidian is the name given to any dark volcanic glass, usually but not always rhyolitic in composition, which has a glassy or satiny lustre and a conchoidal fracture. It is usually rather massive without any phenocrysts, although it may be flow-banded. The white patches shown in the present example are formed by cristobalite, occurring as a high-temperature form of quartz. Pitchstone is another glassy rock of acid composition, differing only from obsidian in its more waxy or resinous lustre, which is perhaps caused by a greater than usual content of water. Both rock types typically occur as lava flows and minor intrusions, such as sills and dykes.

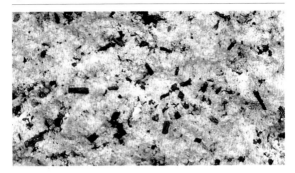

Syenite is a light-coloured, coarse-grained igneous rock, rich in alkalis, composed essentially of alkali-feldspar, including albite, and lesser amounts of sodic plagioclase if present as oligoclase or andesine. Minor amounts of biotite, hornblende, sodic amphiboles (riebeckite) or sodic pyroxenes (aegirine) are present as its ferromagnesian minerals. Syenite differs from granite in the lack of quartz, which always makes up less than 5% of the rock. It becomes a quartz-syenite if quartz is present in greater amounts, up to 10%, passing into granite beyond this limit. Alternatively, nepheline rather than quartz may be present in amounts up to 5%, beyond which the rock becomes a nepheline-syenite.

Larvikite and Monzonite × 0.5

Larvikite is an ornamental variety of coarse-grained syenite which comes from Larvik in the south of Norway. It consists of alkali feldspar, usually anorthoclase, which is a soda-rich variety of microcline, along with sodic plagioclase and other minerals. Polished surfaces show a fine play of blue iridescent colours, reflecting the light internally within the alkali-feldspars as the result of schillerization (German: *schiller*, a play of colours). It is commonly used for shop fronts and other architectural features. The rock becomes a monzonite if sodic plagioclase equals potash feldspar in amount.

Nepheline-syenite (Borolanite)

Nepheline-syenite is a coarse-grained igneous rock composed essentially of alkali-feldspars, together with appreciable amounts of nepheline (usually around 20%), but only small amounts of ferro-magnesian minerals, chiefly sodic amphiboles (riebeckite) or sodic pyroxenes (aegirine). Often difficult to distinguish from quartz, apart from its greasy lustre, nepheline may weather out to form a pitted surface. The rock is usually grey in colour, sometimes tinged green, pink or yellow, unless distinctive blue or yellow grains of sodalite and cancrinite are present. Shown here is borolanite, in which rounded masses of orthoclase and nepheline appear to result from the alteration of leucite phenocrysts, so that they are called pseudoleucites.

Porphyry

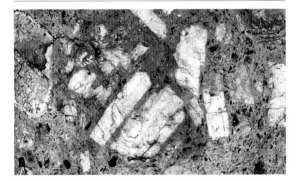

Porphyry is the field-name usually given to the hyperbyssal equivalent of a syenite occurring as a fine-grained but porphyritic rock with feldspar phenocrysts. However, the United States Geological Survey has ruled that the name should only be used as a textural term, prefixed by a rock name to identify its composition, giving granite porphyry for a quartz-porphyry, syenite-porphyry for a feldspar-porphyry, diorite-porphyry for a porphyrite, and so on. The phenocrysts are usually alkali-feldspar, but occasionally sodic plagioclase, typically andesine rather than oligoclase. A feldspar with a rhombic cross-section is known as a rhomb-porphyry.

Trachyte is the volcanic equivalent of a syenite, typically occurring as a fine-grained but often porphyritic rock in lava flows and minor intrusions. It is usually pale-coloured, often weathering whitish or a light grey. The surface may feel rough to the touch, hence its name (Greek: *trachys*, rough). It consists mainly of alkali-feldspar, often found as phenocrysts of high-temperature sanidine. Sodic plagioclase may also be present, together with minor amounts of quartz and ferromagnesian minerals, usually biotite or augite. The groundmass typically consists of feldspar laths, all lying parallel to one another, known as a trachytic texture, formed by the lava continuing to flow as it crystallized.

Phonolite × 4

Phonolite is the fine-grained equivalent of nepheline-syenite, which typically occurs as lava flows and minor intrusions. It consists essentially of alkali-feldspar, often sanidine and anorthoclase, together with varying amounts of nepheline. Amphiboles and pyroxenes of sodic composition, such as aegirine and riebeckite, occur in small amounts. Phonolites are often porphyritic, but the phenocrysts are mostly alkali-feldspar, together with aegirine. The nepheline is often hard to identify, making phonolites difficult to distinguish from trachytes in the field, apart from their darker colour and greasy appearance. Some varieties make a ringing sound when struck with a hammer, hence the name (Greek: *phone*, a sound).

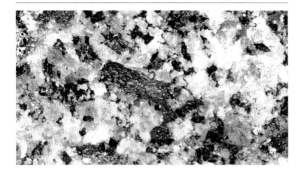

Quartz-diorite is a coarse-grained igneous rock, consisting chiefly of sodic plagioclase and ferromagnesian minerals like biotite, hornblende or augite, together with quartz in amounts greater than 5%. If even more quartz is present, such a rock passes into a tonalite, which is just a granodiorite without any alkali feldspar. Many granite-gneisses of Pre-Cambrian age have such a composition, rather than being true granites. Quartz-diorite and tonalite are more acid rocks than diorite itself, often appearing rather greyish in colour, with lesser amounts of ferromagnesian minerals. Trondhjemite is a quartz-rich tonalite carrying only small amounts of ferromagnesian minerals, chiefly biotite.

Diorites   × 4

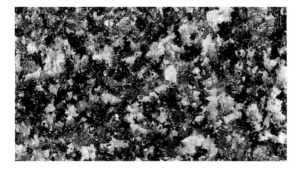

Diorite is a coarse-grained igneous rock of intermediate composition, consisting essentially of sodic plagioclase, usually andesine rather than oligoclase, together with roughly equal amounts of ferromagnesian minerals, such as biotite, hornblende, augite and, rarely, olivine. It typically has a speckled black-and-white appearance, especially if hornblende is present, contrasting markedly with the whitish colour of the plagioclase feldspar (Greek: *diorizo*, distinguish). If present, any small amounts of quartz (less than 5%) are often difficult to distinguish. Although diorites may occur as discrete intrusions in the form of stocks, bosses and dykes, they are often found closely associated with granitic masses.

Appinite

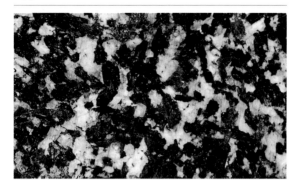

Appinite is a dark-coloured variety of diorite, often with a speckled appearance, in which prismatic crystals of hornblende are very conspicuous, set in a slightly finer-grained matrix of sodic plagioclase, as shown here. It is commonly found associated with kentallenite, which is a dark-coloured, coarse-grained igneous rock, consisting of large crystals of olivine and augite, set in a finer-grained and rather sparse groundmass of biotite, calcic plagioclase and potash feldspar. It occurs along with appinite as a series of minor intrusions around larger masses of granite and granodiorite in the Appin district of the southwest Highlands of Scotland, particularly at Kentallen.

Lamprophyre

Lamprophyre is typically a rather dark-coloured and markedly porphyritic rock of rather basic composition, in which the phenocrysts are all ferromagnesian minerals, such as biotite, hornblende and augite, set in a finer-grained and often altered matrix. Feldspar only occurs in the groundmass of the rock, where alkali-feldspar or sodic plagioclase may be found along with analcite, while biotite, hornblende and augite may also be present. Calcite is frequently present in the groundmass. Lamprophyres usually occur as minor intrusions in the form of dykes and sills, often crowded with xenoliths. The example illustrated is a hornblende-lamprophyre, in which only the phenocrysts remain fresh, unaffected by alteration.

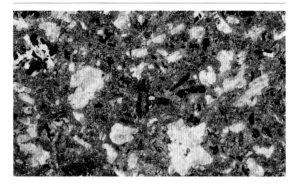

Porphyrite is an intrusive rock of medium grain size with a markedly porphyritic texture, corresponding in composition to diorite and andesite. The conspicuous phenocrysts are typically sodic plagioclase, together with ferromagnesian minerals such as biotite, hornblende and augite, set in a finer-grained matrix of the same minerals. Such rocks usually occur as dykes and other minor intrusions, often associated with major intrusions of granite and granodiorite, and forming dyke-swarms cutting through these plutonic rocks. Shown here is a hornblende-porphyrite with conspicuous phenocrysts of hornblende.

Andesite ×2

Andesite is the volcanic equivalent of diorite, occurring as a dark-coloured and fine-grained but rarely glassy rock in lava flows and minor intrusions. It consists of sodic plagioclase, usually andesine, with roughly equal amounts of ferromagnesian minerals, such as hornblende and augite, or more rarely biotite. All these minerals can occur as phenocrysts if the rock is porphyritic. Its dark-grey or even black colour when fresh makes it difficult to distinguish from basalt, except that it usually weathers to a distinctly purplish crust, rather than forming a brownish crust more typical of basalt. If altered, it often appears purplish or dark mauve throughout the rock.

Gabbro is a rather dark-coloured, coarse-grained igneous rock of basic composition. It is typically composed of calcic plagioclase and pyroxene in roughly equal amounts, so that the rock consists of light and dark minerals, as shown here. The plagioclase feldspar is usually labradorite, although more calcic varieties occur in eucrite. The pyroxene is usually augite, but orthopyroxene may also be present as hypersthene. Such a hypersthene-gabbro merges into norite if hypersthene is the only pyroxene present. Quartz is present in minor amounts in quartz-gabbros, which are often of more acid composition than usual. Likewise, olivine is found in olivine-gabbros, often in quite significant amounts.

Weathered Gabbro ×2

Gabbro often displays a quite different appearance on weathered surfaces, as shown here on the left, since alteration often affects its ferromagnesian minerals like augite and olivine to form a rusty crust to the rock. Its colour is due to the formation of hydrated iron oxides by weathering. Gabbros are also susceptible to alteration, which often occurs throughout the rock, since olivine and hypersthene are often altered to serpentine, while augite becomes changed into chlorite. Calcic plagioclase may also be reduced to aggregates of albite and zoisite by saussurization. All these secondary changes give a rock now appearing much duller in comparison with its unaltered state.

Troctolite and Anorthosite

Troctolite is a gabbro which contains olivine as its only ferromagnesian mineral. Typically, the olivine occurs in green, brown or reddish clusters, studding otherwise greyish rock to give it a speckled appearance, hence its name (Greek: *troktes*, a trout). The rock passes into an allivalite if bytownite or anorthite replaces labradorite as the calcic feldspar. Anorthosite is a light-coloured gabbro which consists essentially of calcic feldspar, usually labradorite or bytownite, containing only a little augite and hypersthene, or occasionally

Troctolite × 2

Anorthosite × 2

olivine. It occurs as distinct layers in gabbroic intrusions, or as large intrusive masses on its own.

Dolerite (or Diabase) ×2

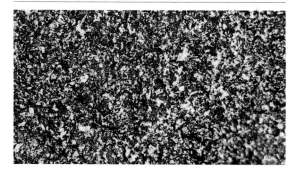

Dolerite (or diabase in North America) is the medium-grained equivalent of gabbro, composed essentially of calcic plagioclase and pyroxene in roughly equal amounts, giving it a mottled appearance. It occurs very widely as large dykes, thick sills and volcanic plugs. It is usually dark grey or black when fresh, typically weathering to a dark brown crust, and often affected by spheroidal weathering. The plagioclase feldspar commonly forms an interlocking meshwork of lath-like crystals. Augite usually occurs as small grains occupying the spaces between the plagioclase laths, but sometimes as larger crystals enclosing the plagioclase laths to give an ophitic texture, occasionally visible in hand specimen.

Basalt

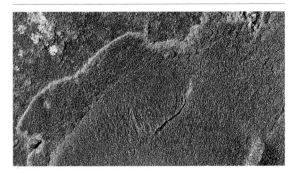

Basalt is the fine-grained equivalent of gabbro or dolerite, and occurs as lava flows and minor intrusions, particularly dykes. It consists of calcic plagioclase, usually labradorite, together with pyroxene in roughly equal amounts as its essential minerals. Pyroxene is usually augite, but hypersthene may occur in the alkali-poor basalts called tholeiites (from Tholey, in Germany). Quartz is common in the groundmass of olivine-free basalts, but only in small amounts. Basalts are usually very fine-grained but still crystalline rocks, often appearing dull on fractured surfaces. They are commonly dark grey or even black in colour when fresh, and often weather to a brownish crust, rich in hydrated iron oxides.

Olivine-basalt

Olivine-basalt contains olivine as well as pyroxene, sometimes forming phenocrysts, but more often restricted to the fine-grained matrix of the rock. The olivine seen in this rock as rounded grains without any crystal outlines is unusually fresh, since it is often altered to serpentine. Olivine never occurs with quartz in the same rock, apart from the iron-rich variety known as fayalite. Otherwise, the two minerals are chemically incompatible, since olivine reacts with quartz to form a pyroxene. Olivine nodules are occasionally found as xenoliths in some basalts, possibly derived from a very deep-seated source in the Earth's mantle.

Porphyritic Basalt

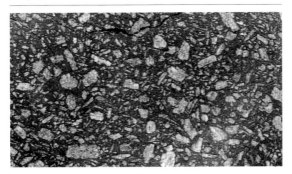

Many basalts are porphyritic, owing to the presence of plagioclase, pyroxene or olivine phenocrysts in the rock, set in a much finer-grained matrix. Plagioclase occurs as whitish-grey crystals, tabular in shape and often more translucent than opaque, which may all lie parallel to one another. Pyroxene can be recognized as black, prismatic crystals with a shiny lustre; while olivine if not altered to serpentine is often found as greenish crystals with a vitreous lustre. Such crystals were formed at depth, before the magma was intruded at higher levels, or erupted from volcanoes, where it cooled more rapidly to give the fine-grained matrix to the rock.

Amygdaloidal Basalt

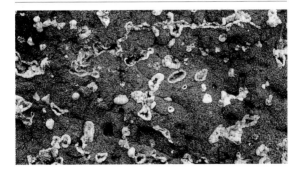

Amygdaloidal basalts have small cavities in the rock which were once gas bubbles, or vesicles, formed by the release of dissolved gases in the magma as it rose towards the Earth's surface, where the pressure was much reduced. Vesicles often become filled with secondary minerals such as chalcedony, opaline quartz, calcite, zeolites or chlorite, forming amygdales (Greek: *amygdalon*, an almond). These minerals were most likely deposited as the lava finally crystallized, while mineral-rich solutions still percolated through the almost solid rock. Such minerals are often more susceptible to the effects of weathering than the surrounding rock, dissolving away to leave empty cavities, just like the original vesicles.

Trap-featuring

Very numerous but highly irregular vesicles give a very slaggy or scoriaceous lava, appearing much like clinker, which often forms the upper portions of basaltic lava flows. A scoriaceous top is often underlain by more solid rock, forming the centre and lower portions of the lava flow, which is less susceptible to weathering. The lava flows exposed on a hillside then erode away in a step-like fashion, forming steeper slopes or even cliffs separated by terraces of flatter ground, which mark the more easily eroded tops of each lava flow or intervening ash beds. The resulting landscape is said to display trap-featuring (from the Swedish *trappa*, a staircase).

Lava-boles

The scoriaceous tops of basaltic lava flows erupted on land are very susceptible to chemical weathering, especially if the climate is hot and humid, and form what are known as lava-boles. This is an ancient term formerly used to describe any earthy material with a yellow, brown or red colour. Larva-boles are deeply weathered residues of bright-red laterite or greyish bauxite. Profound leaching of the original rock leaves behind only hydrated iron oxides and alumina, apart from the occasional core-stones, as its remnants. Such weathering can only have occurred before the lava flow itself was buried by the very next lava flow to be erupted in the volcanic sequence.

Spilite is a basic volcanic rock in which the original minerals have been so altered that the feldspars are now albite, set in a very fine-grained matrix of chlorite, actinolite, epidote and calcite. The rock has a distinctive lime-green colour, appearing much paler than basalt. Spilites commonly retain a basaltic texture or, if they are sufficiently coarse-grained, a doleritic one. They are often associated with kerato-phyre, which is a soda-rich rhyolite or trachyte consisting mainly of albite or oligoclase, together with quartz, chlorite, epidote and calcite, together with phenocrysts of quartz in quartz-keratophyre. Shown here is a volcanic breccia, formed by fragments of spilite.

Pillow-lava   Field of view 2m

Spilites typically occur as pillow-lavas, where the lava flows consist of a jumbled mass of rounded pillows. Rarely more than a metre across, each pillow is encased in very fine-grained or even glassy lava, which encloses an interior of rather coarser-grained rock. The pillows owe their origin to the quenching of molten lava by sea water during sub-marine eruptions. Tongues of molten lava escape through fractures in the lava flow, each swelling into a pillow-like mass until their glassy carapace cools down and solidifies in contact with the sea water, so preventing further growth. Ever more pillows are formed in this way until all the lava flow eventually solidifies.

Peridotite is an ultrabasic rock of coarse grain size, lacking any feldspar. It consists of magnesium-rich olivine, together with lesser amounts of pyroxene, as well as chromite, garnet and iron ores. Peridotite passes into dunite wherever the rock is more than 90% olivine, while it becomes a pyroxenite if olivine is less than 40%. Peridotites are distinctly heavy rocks, appearing dark green or even black when fresh, owing to the lack of any feldspar. They typically weather to a distinctive reddish-brown crust, often recognizable even at long distances. Dunites vary in colour, often appearing greenish owing to their high content of olivine, if not altered to serpentine.

Serpentine (or Serpentinite)

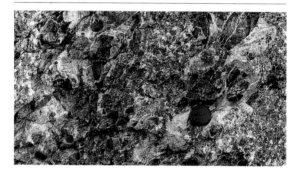

Serpentine is a very distinctive rock, formed by the alteration of ultrabasic rocks, especially in response to movements of the Earth. It consists of serpentine minerals, chiefly chrysotile and antigorite, formed by the hydration and subsequent alteration of olivine and orthopyroxene. Serpentine is usually a dark green rock, often streaked and mottled by more vivid colours. The rock typically appears dull, even waxy and rather compact, especially on fresh surfaces, with a splintery fracture. It is often criss-crossed by narrow veins of fibrous chrysotile. Sheared varieties have rather scaly textures, breaking along smooth and often rather greasy surfaces. Serpentine is often used for ornamental purposes.

PYROCLASTIC ROCKS

Where volcanic eruptions are explosive in nature, fragmental material is often produced, forming the pyroclastic rocks, literally 'broken by fire'. The country-rocks around a volcanic vent, or any solid lava lying within its confines, may be completely shattered, and fragments can then be ejected from the vent by the volcanic explosions. Such pyroclastic deposits accumulate as **agglomerate** if the fragments can easily be seen, but otherwise occur as **volcanic ashes** and **tuffs**.

Ashfall deposits are formed wherever the fragmental material is thrown directly out of the vent by the volcanic explosions, and then falls either to the ground or back into the vent. Typically, the coarser-grained material accumulates nearby, while very fine-grained material is carried away for long distances by the wind.

Ashflow deposits are formed by the explosive eruption of acid lava as its dissolved gases start to escape close to the Earth's surface. This converts the gas-rich lava into an incandescent foam-like mass, which then breaks up into a hot and very turbulent suspension of glass shards and pumice fragments. Capable of flowing downhill for long distances under gravity, such an ashflow eventually comes to rest as an **ignimbrite**, often forming a **welded tuff**.

Agglomerate

Agglomerate is the pyroclastic equivalent of a sedimentary conglomerate or breccia, and is produced by volcanic explosions. It typically consists of fragments of volcanic rocks, greater than 64mm in size, lying in a poorly sorted and fine-grained matrix of volcanic ash or tuff. If the fragments are very angular, the rock is a volcanic breccia. Volcanic bombs are incorporated into such deposits wherever lumps of still-molten lava are thrown into the air by the volcanic explosions. Fragments of country-rocks may also be present. Such rocks are often found as vent-agglomerate lying within a volcanic vent, or immediately around its flanks, where they accumulate to form a volcanic cone.

Volcanic Bombs

Volcanic bombs are incorporated into pyroclastic deposits wherever lumps of molten lava are thrown out of the volcanic vent. As they travel through the air, the bombs take on a variety of different shapes which may be preserved if they are solid or nearly so when they hit the ground. If these molten lumps are fluid they typically adopt a streamlined form, rather like a rugby ball, which is often drawn out into the shape of a slightly twisted spindle with tail-like projections, as they rotate through the air. More viscous lava produces breadcrust bombs, forming rounded lumps with a glassy crust broken up by an irregular network of gaping cracks, as illustrated here.

Volcanic Ash and Tuff   × 4

Volcanic ash is the fine-grained equivalent of agglomerate, generally containing fragments up to 2mm in grain size, which accumulated in a loose and incoherent state. After compaction and subsequent lithification, the indurated rock becomes a tuff. The fragments may consist of fine-grained but still-crystalline rock (lithic tuffs), discrete crystals (crystal tuffs), or glassy particles (vitric tuffs). Volcanic ashes and tuffs commonly contain larger fragments of lava up to 64mm in size, known as lapilli (Latin: *lapilli*, little stones), giving a lapilli-ash or a lapilli-tuff, as illustrated. They are often spherical or ellipsoidal in shape, rather than angular, suggesting that they were ejected in a molten state.

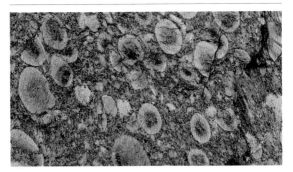

Accretionary lapilli are spherical pellets of volcanic ash, up to several centimetres in diameter, but usually rather less, which typically display a concentric onion-like structure. Their cores may consist of coarse-grained ash, surrounded by a shell of much finer-grained material, or they may be composed wholly of finer-grained ash, forming a series of concentric layers built up around their centres. Whether or not they start to nucleate around solid particles, they most likely result from the accretion of volcanic ash on droplets of water as they condense in a steam-rich eruptive cloud, perhaps forming hailstones. Shown here are accretionary lapilli in a slaty rock, affected by some deformation.

Bedded Ash and Tuff

Volcanic ashes and tuffs are often well-bedded deposits, owing their stratification to the repeated eruption of pyroclastic material from a volcano, and to fluctuations in the explosive force of these eruptions. Typically, such well-bedded rocks are ashfall deposits, formed by the explosive eruption of pyroclastic material from a volcanic vent. The larger fragments accumulate around the vent itself, building up a volcanic cone, while the smaller fragments are deposited at greater distances, falling out of the ash cloud which ascends high above the volcano. Other bedded tuffs accumulate within the vent itself, along with agglomerate, which often just consists of a few larger fragments, as shown here.

Acid Tuff

Pyroclastic rocks can be classified as basaltic, andestic, trachytic, rhyolitic, and so on, according to the overall composition of their fragmental material. However, only agglomerates have fragments large enough to be identified. Tuffs can often only be identified by their general appearance in the field, allowing them to be compared with lavas of the same composition. Usually, only a broad division can be made between basic and acid tuffs, since basic tuffs are often rather dark-coloured rocks with a greenish hue, reflecting the presence of chlorite in a much-altered rock (*see* Bedded Ash and Tuff, page 107), while acid tuffs are usually lighter and much less altered, as shown here.

Welded Tuff (Ignimbrite) × 1

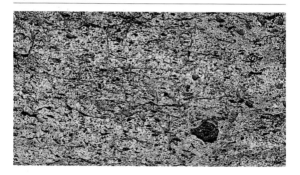

Welded tuffs are ashflow deposits, typically rhyolitic in composition, in which glass shards and pumice fragments are welded together into a solid rock. The pumice fragments collapse under the weight of the overlying material into elongate wisp-like lumps with ragged ends, lacking any vesicles, known as *fiamme* (Italian, a flame). Their presence serves to distinguish such rocks from rhyolite lavas, which they otherwise resemble. Deposited by *nuée ardentes* (French: glowing clouds), welded tuffs are formed by the eruption of pumice fragments and glass shards at a high temperature, together with crystals and rock fragments, supported in a turbulent suspension of hot and ever-expanding gases.

METAMORPHIC ROCKS

Metamorphism occurs deep below the Earth's surface, wherever solid rocks are so altered that they take on quite a different character. Such changes may simply occur in response to the heat given off by igneous intrusions. Existing minerals often recrystallize, and new minerals may grow as a result of chemical reactions in the solid rock, so changing its texture and original mineralogy, but not its chemical composition. **Contact** or **thermal metamorphism** typically occurs wherever such changes affect an aureole of country-rocks around an igneous intrusion.

Metamorphism is often much more pervasive in its effects, especially where sedimentary and igneous rocks are caught up by mountain-building. This is often accompanied by intense deformation which completely alters their structural features as well. Since these changes typically affect rocks exposed over very wide areas, they come under the heading of **regional metamorphism**.

Finally, intense fracturing and granulation, coupled with recrystallization, can affect the rocks lying adjacent to fault-planes, along which movements have taken place, giving rise to **dislocation metamorphism**.

Quartzites, marbles and hornfelses The names given to metamorphic rocks are relatively simple, reflecting their texture and mineralogy, as developed in different sedimentary and igneous rocks. Sandstones and limestones often just recrystallize to form **quartzites** and **marbles**. Shales and mudstones are much more susceptible, being converted by contact metamorphism into a **hornfels**, differing in its mineralogy from the original rock.

Slates, phyllites and schists The regional metamorphism of shales and mudstones produces quite different rocks. Deformation at low temperatures converts such rocks into **slates**, which then pass into **phyllites** as the temperature increases. Under even higher temperatures, slates and phyllites pass into crystalline **schists**.

Gneisses Coarser-grained rocks than schists are produced at greater depths within the Earth's crust, giving rise to **gneisses**, which often underlie all the other rocks of a particular region, so forming a **basement complex**.

Metamorphic minerals Metamorphism typically produces quite distinctive minerals, which often occur as large and well-formed **porphyroblasts**, set in a finer-grained matrix. They include **garnet** and **staurolite**, found in many schists, as well as **cordierite** and **andalusite** in hornfelses. **Kyanite** and **sillimanite** are the other polymorphs of andalusite, formed under higher pressures and temperatures in schists and gneisses.

The mineralogy of metamorphic rocks reflects the intensity of the metamorphism, as defined by their **metamorphic grade**. This is determined by the presence of **index-minerals**, such as chlorite, biotite, garnet, staurolite, kyanite and sillimanite, each appearing in turn as the temperature rises.

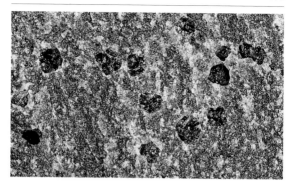

Hornfels is a tough, hard, fine-grained and massive rock, often displaying a purplish tinge but lacking any obvious structure, formed by the thermal metamorphism of shales, mudstones and slates within the contact-aureole of an igneous intrusion. Its matrix is composed of quartz, feldspar and mica, often too fine-grained to be identified. If present, cordierite, andalusite, garnet and sillimanite usually form larger grains with ragged outlines, often weathering out to give a pitted surface. Any cleavage originally present has nearly always been destroyed, although bedding may still be visible. Shown here is a garnetiferous hornfels.

Porcellanite　　　　　　　　　　　　　Field of view 60cm

Porcellanite is an extremely fine-grained and very splintery rock with a conchoidal fracture. Formed by the thermal metamorphism of shales and mudstones, it is usually found as a thin veneer of contact-altered rock, lying along the contacts of minor intrusions, such as dolerite sills and dykes. The metamorphism is apparently caused by the very rapid rise in temperature caused by such an igneous intrusion which, however, lacks sufficient heat to affect more than a very narrow aureole of its country-rocks. Where even more extreme temperatures are reached, actual melting may occur to form a glassy rock known as a buchite.

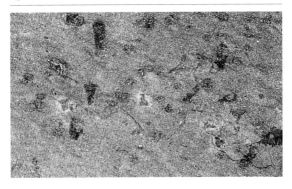

Spotted slate was once a shaly or slaty rock, in which conspicuous spots are now developed by thermal metamorphism. These ovoid or rounded spots may be graphite-rich aggregates, or they may be formed by the incipient growth of crystals, particularly biotite, cordierite, andalusite and chloritoid. The rock itself still splits along its cleavage. It is commonly black, grey, purple or greenish in colour, just like the slate from which it was formed. Spotted slates are found in the outer parts of contact-aureoles around igneous intrusions, passing into more massive hornfelses closer to the intrusion, as recrystallization increasingly destroys their original cleavage.

Chiastolite-slate and Andalusite-schist

Chiastolite-slate is a contact-altered rock midway in character between a spotted slate and an andalusite-schist. As has already been described, chiastolite is a variety of andalusite with carbonaceous inclusions, forming a cruciform pattern within each crystal. It typically occurs as very elongate prismatic crystals, set in a finer-grained matrix, which despite the name of the rock lacks a conspicuous cleavage. An increase in metamorphic grade causes chiastolite-slates to pass into andalusite-schists. Andalusite then occurs as well-developed porphyroblasts, often cut-

Above: *Chiastolite-slate* × 0.33
Below: *Andalusite-schist* × 0.7

ting across the slaty cleavage before it becomes totally obscured by recrystallization, or it is converted into a schistosity by deformation.

111

Slates

Slate is a fine-grained metamorphic rock which splits easily into very thin sheets along a slaty cleavage, lying oblique to the bedding. It is formed by the parallel alignment of micaceous minerals, particularly sericite and chlorite, which occurs in response to compression during low-grade regional metamorphism. Slates are typically formed from sedimentary rocks like shales and mudstones, together with volcanic ashes and tuffs. They vary in colour from black slates, rich in pyrite and graphite (a crystalline form of carbon), through grey, green, blue and purple varieties. The cleavage surfaces are dull-looking, lacking the lustrous appearance more typical of phyllites.

Phyllite   × 1

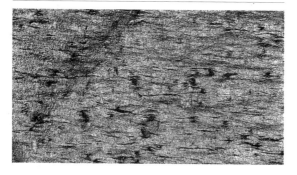

Phyllite is a low-grade metamorphic rock, intermediate in grain size between a slate and a schist. It typically has a well-developed cleavage or foliation, rather than a schistosity. The cleavage surfaces have a silky sheen, owing to the presence of well-crystallized but still very fine-grained micas and chlorite within the rock. Often, they are crumpled by later movements, giving rise to stain-slip cleavages, lying at an angle to the slaty cleavage. Phyllites are often coloured green by chlorite. Phyllonite (*see* page 124) has a similar appearance, but its low-grade nature is a result of retrograde metamorphism, which typically affected higher-grade schists and gneisses under conditions of declining temperature.

Schists

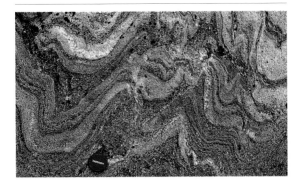

Schist is a regionally metamorphosed rock, in which platy minerals like muscovite, chlorite and biotite all lie roughly parallel to one another. This forms a schistosity rather than a slaty cleavage, along which the rock splits most easily. Typically, the micas and other minerals in the rock are all clearly visible to the naked eye, giving the rock a glistening appearance, quite different from the silky lustre shown by phyllites. The schistosity usually follows the bedding, as marked by any compositional banding within the rock. It is often folded and crenulated, as nearly all schists have been subjected to a long and complex history of deformation and metamorphism.

Mica-schist ×2

Mica-schists are among the most common of all metamorphic rocks, found wherever the temperature and pressure is not high enough for garnet and other metamorphic minerals such as staurolite, kyanite and sillimanite to form in the rock, or where its chemical composition does not favour their formation in response to such temperatures and pressures. Mica-schists therefore occur in passing from such low-grade rocks as slates and phyllites into higher-grade terrains, defined by the presence of these metamorphic minerals. Biotite and muscovite are often found together, along with chlorite if the metamorphic grade is relatively low, while quartz and feldspar make up the rest of the rock.

Garnet-mica-schist

Garnets are commonly found as very conspicuous porphyroblasts in mica-schists, formed by the regional metamorphism of shale or mudstone. They are usually reddish-brown in colour, occurring as the iron-rich variety known as almandine. The crystals may have rounded outlines, or occur as well-formed crystals, as seen here. Such crystals typically occur as rhombic dodecahedra with twelve faces, or more complex forms, which are often found in combination with one another. Such garnets are often altered into chlorite. This occurs as spots and larger aggregates with a dirty green colour. If these still retain the original outlines of the garnet crystals, they are known as pseudomorphs.

Staurolite-schist

Shaly rocks of a suitable composition, rich in iron oxides but lacking much potash, often contain staurolite if they are affected by regional metamorphism under high enough temperatures. The staurolite typically occurs as porphyroblasts, lying in a schistose matrix of quartz, feldspar, muscovite and biotite. It varies in colour from brown to nearly black, sometimes appearing reddish-brown or even yellowish-brown, with a vitreous or somewhat resinous lustre. The crystals are prismatic in habit, sometimes occurring as cruciform twins. They are often found associated with garnet and kyanite, but their brown colour and crystal form are distinctive, especially if twinning is present.

Kyanite-schist

Kyanite-schist is a high-grade metamorphic rock, formed by the regional metamorphism of shaly rocks under conditions of high temperature and pressure, corresponding to depths of many kilometres within the Earth's crust. Occurring as distinctive blue crystals with flattened cross-sections, the kyanite often forms elongate porphyroblasts, lying in the schistosity, unless it is present as clusters and knots of bluish crystals with bladed outlines. It also occurs in quartz veins cutting across such rocks. It is often associated with other metamorphic minerals, such as garnet and staurolite, while quartz, feldspar, muscovite, biotite and mica make up the schistose matrix of the rock.

Sillimanite-schist

Sillimanite grows at the very highest grades of regional metamorphism, replacing kyanite as the temperature rises, just as kyanite took the place of garnet and staurolite at lower grades. Sillimanite-bearing schists (and gneisses) are thus found occupying the very cores of metamorphic belts, along with granites and migmatites, flanked by kyanite and staurolite schists, and then by garnet-mica-schists and other lower-grade rocks. Sillimanite-schists are typically coarse-grained rocks, lacking a perfect schistosity, in which the sillimanite is often difficult to identify, wherever it occurs as a felted mass of extremely fine needles. Garnet and staurolite may also be present, along with biotite, muscovite, quartz and feldspar.

Greenschist

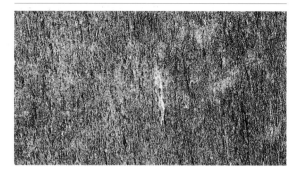

Greenschist is the name given to any schistose rock of low grade, formed by the regional metamorphism of a basic igneous rock, such as basalt or dolerite (diabase). Its greenish colour reflects the presence of chlorite, actinolite and epidote in the rock, which occur along with sericite, sodic plagioclase, quartz and calcite. These minerals are usually too fine-grained to be identified, except that flakes of chlorite may be distinguished from thin needles of greenish actinolite. The schistosity is usually rather crude and irregular, quite unlike a typical slaty cleavage. Greenschists are commonly found interbedded with other regionally metamorphosed rocks of low grade, such as slates, phyllites and chlorite-muscovite-schists.

Epidiorite

Epidiorite is a massive variety of greenschist, consisting of much the same minerals but lacking any form of schistosity or cleavage. It is usually a rather coarse-grained rock, in which the original pyroxenes have been altered into fibrous masses of pale-green amphibole, and the feldspars changed into a more sodic plagioclase, forming fine-grained aggregates of epidote and clinozoisite, together with sericite and calcite, as by-products. Often, igneous textures are preserved in the rock, showing that it has not been affected by deformation. They typically occur as intrusive masses, following the bedding of the surrounding rocks, suggesting they were originally intruded as dolerite sills, often of considerable thickness.

Amphibolite is the higher-grade equivalent of epidiorite, formed by the regional metamorphism of basic igneous rocks. It is typically a much darker green rock than epidiorite, sometimes even black, consisting chiefly of hornblende with varying amounts of plagioclase feldspar. If abundant, the paler feldspar gives a speckled or streaky appearance to the rock. Almandine garnet is often present as dark-red porphyroblasts. Amphibolites vary from rather massive rocks without any schistosity or foliation to more schistose varieties, known as hornblende-schists, in which the hornblende crystals are all aligned parallel to one another. They occur along with garnet-mica-schists and other metamorphic rocks of moderate to high grade.

Glaucophane-schist $\times$ 2

Glaucophane-schist is a distinctive rock, sometimes known as a blue-schist, produced under conditions of great pressure at relatively low temperatures. It typically has a dark blue or even purplish colour, given to it by glaucophane, which is a sodic amphibole. Quartz, albite, chlorite and garnet are the other minerals present, together with dark green jadeite (a sodic pyroxene), lawsonite (a hydrated mineral resembling epidote) and pumpellyite (another hydrated mineral like lawsonite, but rather more complex). Glaucophane-schists are formed at great depths in the Earth's crust by the high-pressure metamorphism of basic igneous rocks, such as dolerites and basalts, together with sedimentary rocks like greywackes.

Marbles

Marble is a metamorphosed limestone, still consisting chiefly of calcite although other minerals may be present. It typically displays a rather granular texture, whether it is a product of regional or thermal metamorphism. If it is deformed, a weak schistosity may result from the parallel alignment of elongate grains. Marble is usually a whitish or greyish rock, particularly the ornamental varieties used for statuary, but its colour can vary greatly, depending on what impurities are present in the rock. Some varieties are coloured black by graphite, occurring as minute inclusions within the calcite grains. Typically, marble weathers much like limestone, giving rise to similar features in the landscape.

Serpentine-marble

Many different marbles are formed by the metamorphism of impure limestones and dolomites, especially if quartz and clay minerals were originally present in the rock. Among the minerals found in such rocks are periclase MgO, brucite $MgO.H_2O$, wollastonite $CaSiO_3$, zoisite $Ca_2Al_3Si_3O_{12}(OH)$, phlogopite $KMg_3AlSi_3O_{10}(OH,F)_2$, tremolite $Ca_2(Mg,Fe)_5(Si_4O_{11})(OH)_2$, grossular garnet $Ca_3Al_2Si_3O_{12}$, idiocrase $Ca_{10}(Mg,Fe)_2 Al_4Si_9O_{34}(OH,F)_4$, diopside $CaMg (Si_2O_6)$ and forsterite Mg_2SiO_4. Forsterite as the magnesia-rich variety of olivine often becomes hydrated to form serpentine, giving a very distinctive rock, displaying irregular patches and streaks of green serpentine in an otherwise pale-coloured rock, as shown here.

Calc-silicate Rocks

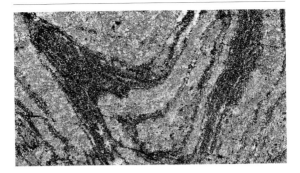

Calc-silicate rocks are metamorphic rocks consisting entirely of silicates rich in lime and magnesia, such as those listed in the entry below left. They are formed wherever all the calcite in an impure limestone is consumed in producing these various minerals. Typically, they occur as fine-grained aggregates of various calc-silicate minerals such as epidote, zoisite, tremolite and calcic plagioclase, often displaying a pale lime-green colour. Diopside, garnet, wollastonite and idiocrase occur at higher temperatures, making irregular patches and discrete grains in an otherwise fine-grained rock. The calc-flintas of Devon and Cornwall are very fine-grained rocks with a flinty appearance, richer in feldspar than other calc-silicate rocks.

Garbenschiefer

× 0.5

The metamorphic rock known in German as garbenschiefer (from German: *garben*, sheaves) can be derived from impure calcareous rocks, or from igneous rocks of basic composition. It is distinguished by the presence of radiating sheaves of very elongate crystals of amphibole, all lying within the schistosity of the rock. These crystals only grew in the schistosity once the deformation affecting the rock had finished. Their stellate character, all radiating from a single point, suggests that they were initially difficult to nucleate, but that once this happened, they grew rapidly. They evidently found it easier to grow along the schistosity, compared to any other direction within the rock.

119

Quartzite is a metamorphic rock composed almost entirely of quartz, formed by the recrystallization of a quartz-rich sandstone, and consisting of an interlocking mosaic of quartz grains, all tightly welded together. Although a metamorphic rock, it resembles a quartz-cemented sandstone (or orthoquartzite). Its detrital nature is often only revealed by the presence of feldspar grains (or other distinctive grains such as blue quartz). Quartzite often fractures along a multitude of very smooth joint-planes, displaying a polished appearance, which cut across the individual quartz-grains in the rock. Quartzites are usually white or pale grey, but sometimes pink or even reddish. Sedimentary structures, especially cross-bedding, may be preserved.

Quartzo-feldspathic Granulite × 1

Quartzites pass into quartzo-feldspathic granulites as their original composition changes, giving a rock in which quartz is accompanied by appreciable quantities of feldspar, usually potash feldspar and sodic plagioclase, together with minor amounts of muscovite or biotite. The name given to such a rock refers to its granular texture, rather than its mineral composition (*see* Pyroxene-granulite, page 122). Lacking a conspicuous schistosity, the rock is often rather massive with an even-grained texture. Such rocks are formed by the regional metamorphism of impure feldspathic sandstones. They pass into quartz-mica-schists if mica is sufficiently abundant for a schistosity to develop.

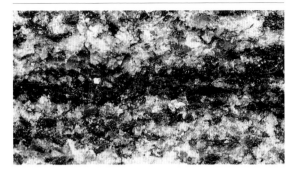

Gneiss is a coarse-grained metamorphic rock which lacks a well-developed schistosity, but which displays a distinct banding or layering on a small scale. Known as a foliation, it is formed by the segregation of granular minerals like quartz and feldspar into distinct but rather irregular layers, separated by other layers, rich in platy or prismatic minerals such as biotite and hornblende. Gneisses may be formed from sedimentary or igneous rocks. Paragneisses of sedimentary parentage can be recognized by the presence of aluminous minerals like kyanite, sillimanite or cordierite in the rock, while the mineral composition of orthogneisses commonly resembles the igneous rocks from which they were formed.

Migmatite

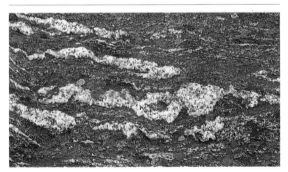

Migmatite is the name given to any coarse-grained gneiss or schist that consists of a metamorphic host-rock, penetrated in a very intricate fashion by irregular and often discontinuous veins of granitic material. Migmatites are found only in high-grade metamorphic terrains, where they often appear to pass into larger bodies of granitic rock, while they are flanked by zones of high-grade schists and gneisses, often sillimanite-bearing. They most likely are formed by the partial melting of their host-rocks in response to extreme metamorphism under very high temperatures. This would at first produce a melt of granitic composition, which could then be injected as granitic veins into the surrounding rocks.

Pyroxene-granulite is a coarse-grained basic rock consisting of pyroxene and calcic plagioclase, often with some garnet, and banded like other gneisses. The pyroxene is typically hypersthene, although clinopyroxene may also be present. The feldspar often appears dark with a greasy lustre. Devoid of any hydrous minerals like biotite or hornblende, pyroxene-granulites are thought to form by the deep-seated metamorphism of basic igneous rocks under temperatures and pressures that favour the crystallization of anhydrous minerals like pyroxene and garnet. They are found exposed in basement complexes, representing the deepest levels of the continental crust. More acid varieties are known as charnockite or hypersthene-granite.

Eclogite   × 2

Eclogite is a very distinctive rock, formed by metamorphism under extreme pressures and quite high temperatures, deep within the Earth. It is typically a coarse-grained and massive rock of unusually high density, consisting of the bright-green sodic pyroxene known as omphacite, and a red garnet belonging to the pyrope-almandine series. Although it shares the same composition as gabbro, or its finer-grained equivalents such as basalt, there is never any feldspar in the rock. Eclogite is commonly found as disrupted masses, forming isolated blocks and lenses in peridotites and serpentines, derived from much greater depths within the Earth. It is commonly used as an ornamental stone for shop-fronts.

Fault-breccia is formed when rocks undergo mechanical breakdown or cataclasis along fault-zones, which are fractures in the Earth's crust, along which movements have occurred. Formed under low pressures close to the Earth's surface, it consists of angular fragments of the wall-rocks, shattered and broken by the fault movements. They may be set in a finer-grained matrix of broken-down material or cemented together by vein minerals such as quartz, calcite, dolomite and barytes. Movements of long duration can result in intensely brecciated rocks in which the fragments are greatly reduced in size. Fault-gouge is a very fine-grained fault-rock, displaying a gritty texture when dry, but which becomes soft and sticky when wet.

Mylonite

Mylonite is an extremely fine-grained rock found along major fault-zones. It is a hard and splintery rock, often rather dark with a flinty texture, and differs from other fault-rocks of a similar grain size by possessing a distinct platiness, along which the rock splits easily. This often becomes a well-developed banding or layering, marked by slight differences in mineral composition or grain size. Mylonites are not just the product of mechanical breakdown, as originally thought, since it is now recognized that the crystal lattices of the original grains become so distorted that they recrystallize to produce innumerable much smaller grains. Further recrystallization may produce blastomylonites, which are coarser-grained than true mylonites.

Flinty Crush-rock and Pseudotachylyte

Flinty crush-rock is a variety of mylonite which has undergone a degree of partial melting in response to the frictional heat generated by the fault movements. It is a black flinty rock lacking any structural features, but showing incipient traces of crystallization under a high-powered microscope. It typically occurs as thin veins and stringers cutting the wall-rocks adjacent to mylonitic fault-zones. Such rocks pass into pseudotachylyte wherever they take on an intrusive habit, occurring as branching veins of black glassy rock, now often recrystallized, which are found cutting the wall-rocks of major fault-zones. They often enclose angular fragments of their wall-rocks, so forming a pseudotachylyte breccia, as shown here.

Phyllonite ×2

Phyllonite is a fine-grained rock resembling a phyllite, formed by the retrograde metamorphism of coarser-grained rocks. Such chlorite-rich rocks are often associated with major fault-zones, where high-grade schists and gneisses have been affected by shearing movements as the temperature falls. They typically have a crude schistosity or foliation rather than a slaty cleavage, and the rock is often intensely contorted and crenulated. Relict grains of such higher-grade minerals as garnet, staurolite and kyanite, set in a chlorite-rich matrix, are a common feature of such rocks, even if they can rarely be identified in the field. The rock shown here consists of quartz-rich lenticles, cut by chlorite-rich shear zones.

Flaser-gneiss is the name given to any coarse-grained igneous rock, usually a gabbro, in which shearing movements have isolated lenticular masses of the original rock. They are enclosed by trails of finely crushed and often recrystallized rock, winding braid-like around these lenticles. They repeatedly divide and then rejoin to form an anastomosing network of shear zones, cutting across the rock. These shear zones typically affect the more easily deformed minerals in the rock, while the intervening lenticles of unaltered rock are formed by minerals which resist deformation most effectively, such as feldspar. Such rocks pass into augen-gneisses, if the matrix has undergone a greater degree of recrystallization.

Augen-gneiss

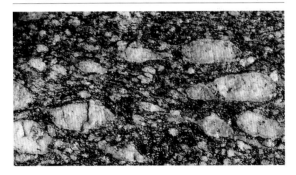

Augen-gneiss is a coarse-grained metamorphic rock, in which large grains of feldspar, or aggregates of quartz and feldspar grains, are present as lenticular augen (German: *augen*, eyes), set in a finer-grained matrix of darker rock. The gneissose foliation displayed by the surrounding rock is deflected around these larger grains, so emphasizing their eye-like appearance. Many augen-gneisses appear to form by the cataclastic breakdown of porphyritic granites in shear zones, particularly as feldspar is more resistant to such deformation than quartz and mica. The feldspar phenocrysts are left as distinct augen in the rock, while the other constituents become much reduced in grain size, as they undergo granulation and recrystallization.

Further reading

Audubon Society Field Guide to North American Fossils. Adolf Knopf, 1982.

Audubon Society Field Guide to North American Rocks and Minerals. Adolf Knopf, 1978.

British Caenozoic Fossils. British Museum (Natural History), London, 1982.

British Fossils, by J. Thackray. Her Majesty's Stationery Office, London, 1984.

British Mesozoic Fossils. British Museum (Natural History), London, 1982.

British Palaeozoic Fossils. British Museum (Natural History), London, 1982.

British Regional Geology (Series). British Geological Survey, Her Majesty's Stationery Office, London.

Cambridge Guide to the Earth, by D. Lambert. Cambridge University Press, Cambridge, 1988.

Challinor's Dictionary of Geology (6th Edition), edited by A. Wyatt. University of Wales Press, Cardiff, 1987.

Concise Oxford Dictionary of Earth Sciences, by A. & M. Allaby, (1990). Oxford University Press, Oxford & New York, 1990.

Field Description of Igneous Rocks, by R.S. Thorpe & G.C. Brown. Geological Society of London Handbook, Open University Press, Milton Keynes, 1985.

Field Description of Sedimentary Rocks, by M.E. Tucker. Geological Society of London Handbook, Open University Press, Milton Keynes, 1982.

Geological Science, by A. McLeish. Blackie & Son, Glasgow, 1986.

Geologists' Association Guides (Series). Geologists' Association, London.

Geology and Scenery in Britain, by J.B. Whitlow. Chapman & Hall, London, 1992.

Introduction to Geology, by H.H. Read & J. Watson. Macmillan Press, London, 1970.

Macmillan Field Guide to Geological Structures, by J.L. Roberts. Macmillan Press, London & Basingstoke, 1989.

Pattern of English Building, by A. Clifton-Taylor. Faber & Faber, London, 1972.

Penguin Dictionary of Geology, by D.G.A. Whitten, & J.R.V. Brooks. Allen Lane, London, 1978.

Elements of Mineralogy, by F. Rutley. Allen and Unwin, London, 1988.

Evening classes and field courses provide an excellent introduction to geology, including the practical identification of rocks, minerals and fossils, while there are numerous field-guides to local geology published by the British Geological Survey, various geological societies, especially the Geologists' Association, and commercial publishers.

Index

127